OPERATING IN THE COURTS OF HEAVEN TO CLEANSE YOUR BLOODLINE

Destiny Image Books by Robert Henderson

Operating in the Courts of Heaven

Receiving Healing from the Courts of Heaven

Unlocking Destinies from the Courts of Heaven

Accessing the Courts of Heaven

Prayers and Declarations that Open the Courts of Heaven

The Books of Heaven

ROBERT HENDERSON

OPERATING IN THE COURTS OF HEAVEN TO CLEANSE YOUR BLOODLINE

CANCEL THE ENEMY'S CASE AGAINST YOU, YOUR FAMILY & YOUR FUTURE

DESTINY IMAGE® PUBLISHERS, INC.
P.O. Box 310, Shippensburg, PA 17257-0310

"Publishing cutting-edge prophetic resources to supernaturally empower the body of Christ"

This book and all other Destiny Image and Destiny Image Fiction books are available at Christian bookstores and distributors worldwide.

For more information on foreign distributors, call 717-532-3040.

Reach us on the Internet: www.destinyimage.com.

ISBN 13 TP: 978-0-7684-7846-4

ISBN 13 eBook: 978-0-7684-7847-1

For Worldwide Distribution, Printed in the U.S.A.

4 / 26

CONTENTS

INTRODUCTION

When I first began to discover the reality of the *Courts of Heaven,* it was related to the whole issue of ancestral sin. I had always had a sense that something was very important with regard to this idea. I had watched people try to get free. I had witnessed them seeking to receive healing. I saw people yearning for deliverance and other realms of needs and breakthrough. They would come in genuine faith and desire. However, they seemed unable to get what God clearly had promised in His Word. This confused me and caused me to question things. I wasn't questioning my faith. I was asking questions concerning what I was missing. Why did people not get lasting results? Then I had my own experience. This was to change me and instruct me in the ways of the Lord. It would unlock for me understanding that would bring breakthrough. This would affect my life but also the lives of many others.

I realize there are many who think that generational curses, bloodline cleansing, and iniquity in the bloodline have no bearing on New Testament believers. In fact, some of these people become angry even at the insinuation that such things could exist. This is why I adopted a saying for those who want to contend with me. I tell them, *"If what you are doing is working for you, then just keep doing that. However, if you haven't gotten breakthrough, you might consider what I'm saying."* The reason I tell them this is because I know their anger is a defense mechanism. What they would like to believe is being threatened. In particular, their reliance on the *false grace message* is being attacked in their own conscience. They know that there are issues that they can't seem to get resolved in their lives. Deep in their spirit man, they realize it *isn't working!*

The false grace message is the idea that Jesus' work on the cross allows us to live any kind of life we want and be okay with Him. His work is so complete that nothing is required of me except some mental assent called *believing*. I am free to follow my own lusts and fleshly appetites. They believe there will be no present-day or eternal consequences. This is because they are convinced Jesus did everything for us. However, real faith always has action attached to it. Plus, when someone is truly *born again* they receive a new nature that desires holiness and purity. A real believer cannot participate in sin and be happy and content. First John 3:9 tells us that when someone is born of God, the seed or nature of God is in them.

> *Whoever has been born of God does not sin, for His seed remains in him; and he cannot sin, because he has been born of God.*

We are told that we *do not sin* when His nature is in us. Obviously this doesn't mean we lose the capability to sin. It means that when His nature is in us, we *don't have to sin.* We may choose to sin, but the nature of God in us gives us the power to say *no* to sin. Being born of God creates within us a longing and desire for His holiness and purity. We are told that the grace of God that we received produces this in us.

Titus 2:11-12 tells us the real grace of God will always propels us to holiness.

> *For the grace of God that brings salvation has appeared to all men, teaching us that, denying ungodliness and worldly lusts, we should live soberly, righteously, and godly in the present age.*

Notice that the grace that brings salvation is a grace that teaches us how to say *no* to sin. We are empowered, out of this grace that births His nature in us, to deny ungodliness and worldly lust! I am afraid that the *grace* many have received is *not* the grace that produces salvation. If they think it is okay to live a life of fleshly lust and appetites, then I have to question that grace. Ultimately, the Lord is the judge. We are all in varying states of maturation. However, anyone who has received the real grace that brings salvation will have a yearning for holiness and purity in their life. It doesn't mean they may not fail at times. However, it does mean that should this occur, they are miserable until they repent and get it fixed. The new nature of God in them will not allow participation in sin. It will compel us, out of a love for God, to repent and get things right.

With this said, so much of what people struggle with in their lives can have its roots in ancestral iniquity. Later, we will get into the things that iniquity in our bloodline can produce. Suffice it to be said here that iniquity in the bloodline grants satan a legal right to tempt us in a given area. Iniquity creates a weakness in us for certain sins. These sins then yielded to can produce strongholds that control us. When we know how to deal with what is empowering these sins from our bloodline, we can break the power and go free. Almost all strongholds have their roots in ancestral activity against God!

There are two main areas that we must be able to revoke satan's right to operate against us. They are iniquity in the bloodline and covenants with demons in the bloodline. We will learn how to go into the Courts of Heaven and undo the enemy's right to use these against us. Once these legal rights are revoked, amazing freedom from ancestral issues is enjoyed.

There is so much to be covered in this book. Over the course of the years since my breakthrough, I have learned so much. I want to impart these truths to you. Let's jump in to the Courts of Heaven and get free through legally revoking the devil's power to enslave and entrap. We will go free.

CHAPTER 1

MY STORY

Many reading this book may know a part of my story. However, placing it in context will help you appreciate it more. Mary and I had lived a blessed life. We had walked through some tough places financially and in raising our six kids, but that was normal for many. Over all and in general, we always moved through any adversity and would get to the other side.

Then we began to face what I would classify as an all-out attack. What I mean by this is that problem upon problem began to come. Trouble upon trouble began to be our normal experience in life. We had transitioned from being pastors for 22 years and into a traveling/itinerant ministry. Things had gone well for about three years. We had moved from Waco, Texas, to Colorado Springs, Colorado. Several of our grown children had moved there as well. Our two teenage boys who were still in high school were still living at home. Then the upheaval started. The first thing that occurred was several well-known ministries decided they didn't like me. They began to spread slander and gossip against me. In our move to Colorado Springs, an influential leader in the Body of Christ had placed his stamp of approval on my life and ministry. I had come into alignment with him. Very much like the father placing the coat of many colors on Joseph and the hatred of his brothers against him being revealed, this happened with me. When this leader favored me, many who were previously joined with him began to detest, ridicule, and attack. All sorts of wicked and untrue accusations were leveled at me. They even reported that I had stolen money from the church I had planted and led in Waco, Texas. Of course, none of this was true, yet they spoke it as fact and blemished and sought to destroy my name and reputation.

During this same time, the pastor I had set in place in Waco, Texas, intended to remove me from apostolic authority in the church I had planted. We operated from an apostolic perspective, which allowed that any pastor would function under my authority as the apostolic leader. We believe this to be New Testament order. However, this pastor, whom I had commissioned to lead this church of several hundred, decided he wanted it completely for himself. He began to imply and outright demean me in the eyes of the people. Mixed with this scenario was the fact that his wife was sick with cancer. The natural pity of people toward this man and his attack against me caused great hostility against me from the people of this congregation. It is not too strong a statement to say we were reviled and even hated by those who once had loved us. This church and its connection to me had provided much-needed finances for the ministry and our family, especially in the beginning stages of the traveling/itinerant ministry. Overnight, because of the slander and evil reports, these finances were gone. Things looked bleak and uncertain. The all-out attack against me and my reputation was having financial repercussions.

It then came to light that this man I had trusted and placed in this pastoral setting had been party to stealing away the equity in my house. When we moved to Colorado Springs, our home in Waco was intended to be sold. From this money, we would have been able to pay off our home in Colorado Springs and be debt-free. As a result of a need to do business, I had signed a document allowing this person to renew a note at the bank. I had no problem doing this, because I *trusted* him. Instead of just doing this from the authorization I had given him, however, he also put my house up for collateral. He secured for himself a $125,000 loan with the equity from *my* house. When I later sold the house, I thought I would have money in hand to pay off my home in Colorado Springs. Instead, I was informed by the bank that any profit from the sale would go toward the existing debt of the church. It seemed everything we had was being stolen away. If this wasn't bad enough, things were going to get worse.

My children and family then began to come under attack and be the target. Our son Adam and his wife went through a divorce. They were very successful youth pastors in the Northwest region of our nation. His wife decided she did not want to be the wife of a pastor/minister. She left him and moved back to Texas. She then forbade him from being able to see their two-year-old little girl. He had no real contact with her for more than five years. This was a great heartache and heartbreak to not only Adam, but also to our entire family. Through much wrangling in the natural court system, eventually contact was restored and relationship with the daughter was mended. However, things were in great upheaval.

In this same time period, another son of ours, Mark, got deeply involved in drugs. I knew prophetically that Mark was going to die because of his activities and the people he was involved with. I was praying against this but intuitively knew that his death was imminent. I would arise every morning before dawn and look on the internet news to see if a teenager had died the night before. It was a terrible time of torment and pain. Mark was consistently locked up and jailed by the police on drug-related charges. We spent much money and time bailing him out of jail.

One night, we woke up in the wee hours of the morning with Mark standing in our bedroom. He and his friends had been downstairs in the basement where they slept. The door was open to the outside and police had come in looking for Mark. We woke up with Mark in our bedroom seeking to hide from the police who were now in our home. We spent quite a bit of time convincing the police to leave our home. This is a trauma I will not soon forget. The pain, fear, and shame associated with this were unimaginable. It seemed the gates of hell had been opened against us. I was totally baffled and perplexed over *why* this was happening. I knew nothing of the Courts of Heaven or bloodline cleansing. I thought I must have done something so very terrible that was allowing all this to occur. There seemed to be no answer. No matter how much I prayed, things kept escalating out of control. It was in the midst of all of this that the Courts of Heaven teaching was about to unfold. I was about to encounter revelation that would change my life. It would also have a dramatic effect on the lives of people across the nations.

In this book, I will walk through a chronological timeline of the events that brought this revelation. In the process of this, I will seek to unveil spiritual truth that can be used to secure victory in your life. Let's walk together in this process. There is hope for you and your family. Deliverance can and will be yours!

> Lord, as I come before Your Courts, I bring all the struggles, attacks, and hindrances being brought against me. My purpose is to do Your will in my life. I ask that anything in my bloodline that is working against me legally will now be revealed. Unveil for me anything and everything that would grant the devil the legal right to resist Your purposes in

my life. Show me what might be legally working against me, I pray, in Jesus' Name, amen.

CHAPTER 2

THE LORDSHIP OF JESUS

As the events I described began to transpire in our lives, I had no answer. I was at a loss. We had always been blessed of the Lord. Our home had always been one where Jesus was honored and served. There was no double standard in our lives or family. What we were in public ministry, we were in private devotion. I say this because I had been told and believed that so many problems in families could be traced to *hypocrisy*. This word basically means a *playacting* or *playing a part* for others to see while things are completely different behind the scenes. When this is the reality, eventually there is a destruction that can come. The true nature of things is revealed.

Jesus spoke of this when He spoke of two different houses in Luke 6:46-49. One house was built on sand, while the other house's foundation was on a rock.

> *But why do you call Me "Lord, Lord," and not do the things which I say? Whoever comes to Me, and hears My sayings and does them, I will show you whom he is like: He is like a man building a house, who dug deep and laid the foundation on the rock. And when the flood arose, the stream beat vehemently against that house, and could*

> *not shake it, for it was founded on the rock. But he who heard and did nothing is like a man who built a house on the earth without a foundation, against which the stream beat vehemently; and immediately it fell. And the ruin of that house was great.*

The whole issue in this story was, did the one who heard the words of the Lord practically respond to them? In other words, did they do something with what they heard? In the case Jesus presented, both houses came under the pressure of the storm. One was able to weather the storm, while the other one fell and was destroyed. The whole issue was, is there a foundation under the house? The house can represent an individual, church, business, or most definitely a family!

The question that needs to be asked is, do I have a foundation on the Rock or have I built on the earth without a foundation? Jesus is very clear about how we get a foundation that is on the Rock as opposed to building without one. We don't just do lip service to His Lordship, but actually submit all things to Him and His authority. We line everything up with Him and His word in our lives. Philippians 2:8-11 declares that Jesus is absolute Lord as a result of the place God has given Him. This placement is a result of His complete surrender and submission to God His Father.

> *And being found in appearance as a man, He humbled Himself and became obedient to the point of death, even the death of the cross. Therefore God also has highly exalted Him and given Him the name which is above every name, that at the name of Jesus every knee should bow, of those in heaven, and of those on earth, and of those*

> *under the earth, and that every tongue should confess that Jesus Christ is Lord, to the glory of God the Father.*

Jesus' total obedience to the Father's will resulted in the Father placing Him as Lord of all. This is why we must subjugate ourselves under Jesus' authority. Not just with words, but in actuality. When we do this, we are renouncing all rebellion and acknowledging the place Jesus has by virtue of the Father's choosing.

There are three keys in this scripture in Luke 6 where Jesus admonishes us to walk under His Lordship. We are told we must *come to Him, hear Him, and do what He says* in Luke 6:47.

> *Whoever comes to Me, and hears My sayings and does them, I will show you whom he is like.*

I have found that spending time with the Lord in prayer and worship, hearing His voice, and then obeying, grants great legal place before Him in the Courts of Heaven. My obedience to the Lord in all areas, but especially places where He has specifically instructed me, grants testimony on my behalf. In other words, when I hear the Lord tell me to do something, I must obey Him. This speaks on my behalf before His Courts. When we hear the voice of the Lord speak to us, this is an opportunity for us to gain a place of authority in His Courts. I could give several examples, but let me just mention a couple. I was praying one morning when suddenly I heard the Lord say I would "eat the fat and drink the sweet and send portions to those for whom nothing was prepared." When I heard this, I knew it was from Nehemiah 8:10.

> *Then he said to them, "Go your way, eat the fat, drink the sweet, and send portions to those for whom nothing is*

> *prepared; for this day is holy to our Lord. Do not sorrow, for the joy of the Lord is your strength."*

I understood that this was about me prospering and having the ability and strength to bless and empower others who weren't being taken care of. The part about *"sending portions to those for whom nothing was prepared"* really stood out to me. I knew God wanted to bless me on a significant level and that I was to use a portion of it to finance something that wouldn't be financed otherwise. However, I didn't know what that was. I knew it was the word of the Lord, but didn't know how to proceed. Therefore, I just waited.

About two months later as I was waking up one morning, I was in that state between sleep and awake. As I was lying there, I realized I had dreamed about Arabic girls who could not go to school because of their gender. They were forbidden from an education because they were female. I remember seeing one such girl in my dream. As I was awakening, I suddenly heard these words again: "*Send portions to those for whom nothing is provided.*" I became awake and knew that God was telling me to finance schools for these girls in the Arabic world. I even wondered if I was supposed to start schools in that part of the world. I didn't know how I was to do this, but knew I was supposed to. I only knew one person who ministered in that part of the world, but I didn't know if they did anything like this. Through a process of searching for this person, I found them. It was amazing to find out, when I eventually sat down with them, that they in fact did finance schools for girls. They told me that these girls, without an education, would spend their lives in the *brickyards* making bricks or be trapped in the sex-trade industry. However, with an education, they can have a different future. They are not only taught to read, write, and do math and other subjects, they are also taught to sew and make clothing. Their future is completely changed because of a minimal education.

We are a part of making this happen. We send portions to those for whom nothing would otherwise be provided and prepared. More than this, however, my offering and obedience speaks in the Courts of Heaven for me. When I come before the Courts of Heaven, I can cite this as obedience before the Lord. Not only the fact that I obeyed and am obeying, but the money itself is speaking in the Courts for me too. Hebrews 7:8 clearly unveils that money has a voice before the Courts of Heaven.

> *Here mortal men receive tithes, but there he receives them, of whom it is witnessed that he lives.*

This scripture discloses that when we honor Jesus with our tithe as our High Priest after the order of Melchizedek, that tithe *witnesses* before Him. The word *witness* is the Greek word *matureo.* It means "to testify, be a witness, give evidence." In other words, the money we give releases testimony before the Lord on our behalf. We also see that money has a judicial effect in James 5:4. In this scripture we are told that any money that has been held back that belongs to us is *crying out.*

> *Indeed the wages of the laborers who mowed your fields, which you kept back by fraud, cry out; and the cries of the reapers have reached the ears of the Lord of Sabaoth.*

Notice that it is the held-back wages that belong to someone that are crying out. The word *cry out* literally means to *scream.* When something has been stolen from us, it is crying out against the one who stole it. If you read the whole discourse here, you would find a pronounced judgment against those who have done this unlawful thing. They will suffer consequences, perhaps in this life, but definitely in the one that is to come. All because of the *testimony* of the stolen wages that is *screaming* out in the Courts of Heaven. There are many other scriptures we could look at concerning the voice of money and sacrifice. However, let it be established that money has a great voice in the Courts of Heaven. When I obey the Lord and support what God told me to, my obedience speaks in the Courts of Heaven, as well as the money that is sowed.

Another time I was told by the Lord to do something was in our moving back to Colorado Springs, Colorado. In a dream it was prophetically declared over me that "*this time by the grace of God, I will live at a higher level!*" Much of what I have talked about in Chapter 1 happened in Colorado Springs. In other words, it was a very difficult period in our lives. Yet I was being told to move back to this city. Jesus is our Lord. Therefore, we have obeyed and relocated one more time. It has definitely been a place of His grace for us. Also, we have been given a *seat* in the spirit realm because of our obedience. There have been two different visitations from the Lord where an apostolic place of authority has been given to me. One of these visitations showed that I was now standing in a place in the Courts of Heaven to change things in our nation from this location. Our obedience to move to Colorado Springs allowed the Courts of Heaven to give me this place of grace. I was told in the visitation that we now had what we needed to change things over our nation in the Courts.

The other visitation was from the Cloud of Witnesses. Remember that Hebrews 12:1-2 shows us this dimension in the unseen realm.

> *Therefore we also, since we are surrounded by so great a cloud of witnesses, let us lay aside every weight, and the sin which so easily ensnares us, and let us run with endurance the race that is set before us, looking unto Jesus, the author and finisher of our faith, who for the joy that was set before Him endured the cross, despising the shame, and has sat down at the right hand of the throne of God.*

In that we are *surrounded,* it means that we are in the same dimension that they are in. They are the Cloud of *Witnesses.* This word in the Greek is *martus.* It means a *judicial witness.* It also means a *martyr.* They have a weight of authority in the Courts of Heaven because they laid down their lives while in the earth. This doesn't mean they were physically martyred. It means that they sacrificed their own desires to do the will of God. This has granted them a significant place of glory in the heavenly realm. In the visitation, I had someone from the Cloud of Witnesses come to give me an apostolic place. This person actually gave something to someone when they were alive in the natural. In the visitation, however, they were giving me something from the Cloud of Witnesses. I knew that my move to Colorado Springs had unlocked for me the right to sit in an apostolic seat this person held in Colorado Springs. From the Courts of Heaven and the Cloud of Witnesses, I have legally been granted this place. This all transpired because of my obedience to do what Jesus as Lord had commanded me. My obedience is speaking on my behalf in the Courts of Heaven for God's will to be done in the earth. What an honor to be a part of the process!

A second secret/key to walking under His Lordship is to dig deep. Luke 6:48 let us know that those who lay a foundation are not moved in storms. This laying of the foundation on the Rock requires digging.

> *He is like a man building a house, who dug deep and laid the foundation on the rock. And when the flood arose, the stream beat vehemently against that house, and could not shake it, for it was founded on the rock.*

When we speak of digging deep, it implies to me a searching. The natural digging deep to get to the bedrock means you are looking for it. It is moving everything out of the way to get to what the house might be built on. We know of course that the Rock is Jesus. First Corinthians 10:4 clearly states that Jesus as the Christ is the Rock.

> *And all drank the same spiritual drink. For they drank of that spiritual Rock that followed them, and that Rock was Christ.*

You'll remember that Moses brought water from the Rock twice. Once by obediently striking it and the second time by striking it again in opposition to God's word. This actually cost Moses his right to enter the promised land. However, this established that the Rock is Christ. We are to seek Him and establish our lives on who He is! When we do this, we become immovable and set. The digging deep to find "the Rock" is us coming to progressive revelation of who Jesus is. As we gain more and more revelations of the character and nature of the Lord, we are more securely set upon Him. The storms of life will not have power to move us, because we know who the Lord is in the midst of them. We shall not be moved.

The third key/secret to Jesus being Lord in our lives is to always be *building.* When we examine this scripture in which Jesus is making a distinction between the two houses, we see that the one that fell was *built* while the one that stood was *building.* To help magnify this, let's look at Luke 6:47-49 again.

> *Whoever comes to Me, and hears My sayings and does them, I will show you whom he is like: He is like a man* ***building*** *a house, who dug deep and laid the foundation on the rock. And when the flood arose, the stream beat vehemently against that house, and could not shake it, for it was founded on the rock. But he who heard and did nothing is like a man who* ***built*** *a house on the earth without a foundation, against which the stream beat vehemently; and immediately it fell. And the ruin of that house was great.*

The house that stood was the house that was always in process. In other words, we must always be under construction in our Christian walk. We must allow the Holy Spirit the right to continue to perfect us. This is what we are told in several places. Psalm 138:8 lets us know that God will not forsake us as the works of His hands.

> *The Lord will perfect that which concerns me;*
> *Your mercy, O Lord, endures forever;*
> *Do not forsake the works of Your hands.*

God is faithful to complete what He has started. Sometimes we are afraid we may not make it or measure up. However, if we will maintain a heart that doesn't quit, God will be true to His word. Philippians 1:6 is very clear that God will not stop working on us.

> *Being confident of this very thing, that He who has begun a good work in you will complete it until the day of Jesus Christ.*

God is not going to stop His good work in us until Jesus returns. When we are aware of this, we can agree with and continue to see that work done. We can be in the constant process of *building* rather than having been *built.* May God give us grace to allow the Father, through the Spirit, to complete that which concerns us. May we never sense or feel that we have *arrived.* The apostle Paul never let himself get into that idea. He was always moving forward to the next places in God. Philippians 3:12-15 shows this passion that was maintained in Paul's heart.

> *Not that I have already attained, or am already perfected; but I press on, that I may lay hold of that for which Christ Jesus has also laid hold of me. Brethren, I do not count myself to have apprehended; but one thing I do, forgetting those things which are behind and reaching forward to those things which are ahead, I press toward the goal for the prize of the upward call of God in Christ Jesus.*
>
> *Therefore let us, as many as are mature, have this mind; and if in anything you think otherwise, God will reveal even this to you.*

Paul recognized that he had to be in a constant place of building. He wasn't perfect yet. There were still issues in his life that needed to be ironed out. Notice, however, that this sense of always moving forward flowed from a mindset of *maturity.* Sometimes we think maturity in the Lord is having no remaining issues. This is not true. Paul depicts maturity as that which is always chasing what we were created for. May this mind be in us even as it was in the apostle Paul. When this is in us, we are yielded and submitted to His Lordship. This does speak for us in the Courts of Heaven. We are choosing His ways above our own. May we each come under His Lordship and obey Him fully.

> As I stand before Your Courts, Lord, may it be recorded that I have surrendered and made You the Lord of my life. Let it be known that I don't just say, "Lord, Lord," but I submit myself to You and Your will. May this speak in the Courts on my behalf. Also let it be known that I repent for any place where I have not done Your will. I purpose to fulfill all that You have said, are saying, and will say to me. I yield my life to You completely. In Jesus' Name, amen.

CHAPTER 3

THE REALITY OF GENERATIONAL CURSES

There is a great argument today about the reality of generational curses or iniquity in the bloodline. The question is, can the devil, in New Testament order, cause curses to land against people? Of course, my position is they can. People have been so inundated with the *false grace* message that they believe big portions of scripture no longer apply. In particular, they believe that the Old Testament is completely irrelevant and even a form of bondage now.

The problem is that the earliest apostles, who wrote scripture, cited and used the Old Testament to qualify their arguments for grace. In fact, when they spoke in the New Testament of *scripture,* they were speaking of the Old Testament. Peter declared that scripture was made up of what the apostles were saying and what the prophets of old had said. Second Peter 3:1-2 shows us this principle.

> *Beloved, I now write to you this second epistle (in both of which I stir up your pure minds by way of reminder), that you may be mindful of the words which were spoken*

> *before by the holy prophets, and of the commandment of us, the apostles of the Lord and Savior.*

The prophets who spoke before were from the Old Testament. The commandments of the apostles were a present day revelation. Peter is declaring both make up New Testament importance. Peter even spoke of the more sure word of prophecy, which was the prophets of the Old Testament. Second Peter 1:18-21 shows Peter elevating the Old Testament scripture to a place of dominance.

> *And we heard this voice which came from heaven when we were with Him on the holy mountain.*
>
> *And so we have the prophetic word confirmed, which you do well to heed as a light that shines in a dark place, until the day dawns and the morning star rises in your hearts; knowing this first, that no prophecy of Scripture is of any private interpretation, for prophecy never came by the will of man, but holy men of God spoke as they were moved by the Holy Spirit.*

In referring to the Old Testament scriptures, Peter declares it is a light shining in a dark place. Clearly the early apostles did not think the Old Testament to be irrelevant or useless. We could spend a lot more time on this. Suffice it to say, without the scriptures from the Old Testament, we would not have the New Testament. This was the only scripture the early church had. If we try to make it something of no use today, we are making a grave mistake. The writers of the New Testament drew from the revelation of the Holy Spirit. So much of what they understood came out of the Old Testament. Apollos is spoken of in Acts 18:24-28. He is declared to be mighty in scripture.

> *Now a certain Jew named Apollos, born at Alexandria, an eloquent man and mighty in the Scriptures, came to Ephesus. This man had been instructed in the way of the Lord; and being fervent in spirit, he spoke and taught accurately the things of the Lord, though he knew only the baptism of John. So he began to speak boldly in the synagogue. When Aquila and Priscilla heard him, they took him aside and explained to him the way of God more accurately. And when he desired to cross to Achaia, the brethren wrote, exhorting the disciples to receive him; and when he arrived, he greatly helped those who had believed through grace; for he vigorously refuted the Jews publicly, showing from the Scriptures that Jesus is the Christ.*

What scripture was Apollos mighty in? It was the Old Testament scripture. This was all they had. He preached the revelation of Jesus from the Old Testament. Notice that Apollos showed that Jesus was the Christ from the scriptures. This would have been the Old Testament scriptures. If the Old Testament was applicable in their day, it is still applicable today. We mustn't dismiss understanding from the Old Testament. We need to do what Paul said to Timothy in 2 Timothy 2:15. We are to correctly decipher the word of God.

> *Be diligent to present yourself approved to God, a worker who does not need to be ashamed, rightly dividing the word of truth.*

The word *dividing* is the Greek word *orthotomeo.* It means "to make a straight cut, to dissect." As we read the word, we need the Holy Spirit to help us discern how things are to be applied in our lives. However, we are told that *all* scripture is given by God. Second Timothy 3:14-17 gives us further insight into what scripture is for. Paul is urging Timothy to treat all scripture with reverence and honor.

> *But you must continue in the things which you have learned and been assured of, knowing from whom you have learned them, and that from childhood you have known the Holy Scriptures, which are able to make you wise for salvation through faith which is in Christ Jesus.*
>
> *All Scripture is given by inspiration of God, and is profitable for doctrine, for reproof, for correction, for instruction in righteousness, that the man of God may be complete, thoroughly equipped for every good work.*

Again, this would have been speaking predominately of the Old Testament. Paul is clearly under the impression that *all* scripture is to be accepted as inspired by God. May the Lord help us to come out from under present deceptions and received the full word of God. We cannot dismiss something as irrelevant just because it's part of the Old Testament scriptures.

With this said, how may we connect the dots with regard to bloodline issues and generational curses? There are three main things I would point out that would help us to understand generational issues in a present-day context. First of all, we should know that the Holy Spirit executes into place the work of the cross. Everything Jesus did on the cross was legal in nature. In fact, from the cross there was a judgment rendered against the powers of darkness. John 16:8-11 lets us see that the Holy Spirit has come to set into place the legal work of Jesus.

> *And when He has come, He will convict the world of sin, and of righteousness, and of judgment: of sin, because they do not believe in Me; of righteousness, because I go to My Father and you see Me no more; of judgment, because the ruler of this world is judged.*

Jesus was explaining the work of the Holy Spirit when He was to come. He would deal with the sin of unbelief. He would unveil true righteousness. He would also bring revelation of the judgment of the ruler of this world. The Holy Spirit would empower us to move in agreement with Him, to set the legal work of the cross into place. Without the person of the Holy Spirit, nothing Jesus did on the cross would have application in our lives. Even though the cross caused a verdict to be rendered against satan, it's the Holy Spirit who executes it into place. Only then do we get the benefits of Jesus' work for us on the cross. A verdict not executed into place has no power. This would have been what happened from the cross without the person of the Holy Spirit. This is why we must know how to cooperate with the Spirit of God. Jesus dying on the cross was not enough! We must agree with and move in harmony with the Spirit of the Lord to get what has been legally provided for us. This is why the apostle Paul encourages us in 1 Corinthians 12:1 to not be ignorant of the Holy Spirit's ways.

> *Now concerning spiritual gifts, brethren, I do not want you to be ignorant.*

Paul would continue in his discourse to talk about the different manifestations of the Holy Spirit and how to recognize them. He was seeking to bring understanding of the Spirit's ways of operation. Without this the believers would miss the Holy Spirit's application of the legal work of the cross. Their ignorance could cost them the intent of God being done. If we are to get the benefit of Jesus' legal work, we must know how to agree with what the Spirit is doing. He is here to set in place all that Jesus legally accomplished on the cross. This includes the revoking of legal claims against us in our bloodline. The Holy Spirit takes what Jesus did and, at our confession of faith, revokes satan's legal rights against us. He is here to set into place everything Jesus accomplished legally for us. If we don't know how to agree with the Holy Spirit, even though Jesus legally accomplished it, we will get no benefit from it.

The second issue I want to target is about curses. We know in Galatians 3:13 that we are told curses have been dealt with.

> *Christ has redeemed us from the curse of the law, having become a curse for us (for it is written, "Cursed is everyone who hangs on a tree").*

This tells us that when Jesus hung on the cross and died, we were redeemed from any and every curse. Curses are legal rights for satan to sabotage our success and future. We will deal with this in later chapters. However, according to this scripture we were freed from the power of curses as a result of Jesus becoming a curse for us. This is wonderful. However, Revelation 22:1-3 tells us that in the millennium reign of Christ, there will be *no more curse.*

> *And he showed me a pure river of water of life, clear as crystal, proceeding from the throne of God and of the Lamb. In the middle of its street, and on either side of the river, was the tree of life, which bore twelve fruits, each tree yielding its fruit every month. The leaves of the tree were for the healing of the nations. And there shall be no*

> *more curse, but the throne of God and of the Lamb shall be in it, and His servants shall serve Him.*

Wait a minute. I thought the curse ended at the cross. Yet here we are being told that there will be no more curse only in the rule of Jesus upon the earth. So which is it? Did curses end at the cross or do they end at the millennium rule of the Lord? What is going on here? If we understand what happened at the cross, it is easy to explain. The cross allowed verdicts to be rendered. When we read scriptures like Galatians 3:13, we are reading *a stated verdict of the cross.* It is a statement of what Jesus legally did. Revelation 22:1-3, however, is the execution of that verdict into place fully. Up until the full execution of the verdict into place at Jesus' millennium reign, we must take what Jesus did and through the power of the Holy Spirit execute it into place. Otherwise, we do not get the benefit of Jesus' work for us.

We can be free from curses. However, there will not be a wholesale release from curses until the second coming of Jesus and His reign. In the present, we must move in cooperation with the Spirit of God to get the benefit of what Jesus legally did for us. Through the Holy Spirit we can execute into place the verdict of the cross for ourselves, our families, and the assignments God has given us. There will come a time when all curses will be revoked. Until that time, we must legally annul them through our faith and the power of the Holy Spirit. This is where dealing with bloodline issues comes in.

The third issue to point out is found in Ezekiel 18:1-3. We are told from the Old Testament that there should be no iniquity working against us in our bloodline.

> *The word of the Lord came to me again, saying, "What do you mean when you use this proverb concerning the land of Israel, saying:*
>
> *'The fathers have eaten sour grapes,*
> *And the children's teeth are set on edge'?*
>
> *"As I live," says the Lord God, "you shall no longer use this proverb in Israel."*

This is clearly the Lord declaring that the sins of the fathers should not affect or influence coming generations. Fathers eating sours grapes and children's teeth being set on edge speaks of the right of iniquity to work against us. God is declaring through Ezekiel that this is not what is to occur. Many take this scripture and attack the idea that there are generational curses today. However, let's look at this passage more closely. If we are to really see what is being declared here, we must look at the entire chapter of Ezekiel 18. Clearly the Lord is saying that it is His prophetic intent for the father's sins not to affect the children. However, there can be a prophetic intent without it being seen. If we finish the chapter, we will see what is required for this to be reality. Ezekiel 18:30 shows us what is necessary to get the prophetic desire of God.

> *"Therefore I will judge you, O house of Israel, every one according to his ways," says the Lord God. "Repent, and turn from all your transgressions, so that iniquity will not be your ruin."*

Remember that *iniquity* is the sin that is in the bloodline. We will see this more clearly in later chapters. Notice that the Lord declares they must repent or the sin in the bloodline/iniquity will ruin their future! But didn't the Lord just say that the sins of the fathers weren't to effect the children? Of course He did. This is the Lord's passion and desire. For it to be a reality, the people have to repent so that the iniquity/sins of the fathers will not be legally used against them. I always tell people they have to finish the chapter in Ezekiel 18 to get the full meaning of what God was saying. When we repent for ourselves and the iniquity of the fathers, then our teeth will not be set on edge. We will be free from the ruin and power of iniquity. Generational curses will not have a right to determine our future. We will be freed to come into the destiny arranged and designed by God for us. We can stand in the Courts of Heaven and see every legal claim against us removed. This will result in us having the liberty to experience the goodness of God on every level of our life.

> As I stand before Your Courts, Lord, I call these Courts into remembrance of all Jesus legally did on the cross. I therefore ask according to scripture that every generational issue and curse would be revoked in Jesus' Name. Any legal claim satan is making against me and my family, let it be annulled now. I thank You that Your Word is true. I accept the scriptures as Your final authority. May I know how to rightly divide the word of truth and apply it in Your Courts.
>
> I also ask that the Holy Spirit will empower me to set in place Your judgments against the powers of darkness and the ruler of this world. From Your cross, let these judgments be implemented against all curses. I also request that iniquity would not be my ruin. May my repentance speak in the Courts of Heaven and remove the effects of my father's

sin against me. Let not my teeth be set on edge because of my father eating sour grapes. I declare that Your blood, Lord Jesus, speaks for me and removes any right of the devil to use my father's sin against me. I desire the prophetic promise of God to occur, as my repentance agrees with Your speaking blood. In Jesus' Name, amen.

CHAPTER 4

COVENANTS UNDONE

Even though our family had lived under the Lordship of Jesus and we had been dedicated to His purposes, we were now under tremendous attack. The thing that was not allowing us to fall to pieces was that we were being built in the Rock. However, the attacks were taking their toll. I was praying and doing everything I knew to do to get answers to these situations. Nothing was changing. Everything was spiraling out of control. It seemed that before I could get one problem solved, there were three more to deal with. I had no idea what to do. Everything that had worked for me for the last 25-plus years no longer had an effect. I had been a man of prayer since 1980. I had dedicated myself to daily prayer and had sought the Lord with my whole heart. I had seen many breakthroughs and had stood in amazement at God's direction in our life. Now, however, nothing was working. Every principle I had learned that had worked in previous times seemed to be ineffective now. I didn't know what to do.

At this time in my life, I was invited to travel to another country to minister. I did not know the people who were inviting me. However, I felt that I was to go. As I arrived in this nation where I was to minister, I was greeted and we began to talk. The leader of this ministry then made a statement to me. They said, "We want to cleanse your bloodline." When this was said, I didn't understand what they were talking about. I said in response, "What's wrong with my bloodline?" I'll never forget the response of this leader. They said back to me, "Oh, I'm so sorry. You don't understand. When you stand to minister on my platform, there will be many people from many nations. If there is anything *legal* in you or your bloodline, this will give these demons and principalities the right to come after you and your family." As this was communicated to me, the first thought that went through my mind was, *I've got American demons after me, I don't need demons from other countries after me too.* I immediately said to these people, "Please, cleanse my bloodline."

They then took me into a room with about three or four other people. One was going to lead this bloodline cleansing session, while the others were going to listen and be sensitive to what God might reveal. They began by having me pray a prayer like this.

> Lord, as I come before You, I open my life and bloodline up to You. I ask that anything in me or my bloodline that the devil might use legally against me would be exposed and known. Any place that he would claim legal rights to resist and destroy, let it be known and revealed, in Jesus' Name, amen.

As I prayed this simple prayers, one of the prophetic people there listening said, "I see that someone from Robert's bloodline made a covenant with a demonic god named Parax." I had no idea what they were talking about. I'd never heard anything like that in my life. Even the rest of the people in the room had never heard or seen anything like that happen in any of their sessions. They then pulled out a computer and did a very spiritual thing. They Googled *parax.* The results of the search were to be life-changing for me. It was found that Parax was a demon god whose chief characteristic was to *suck dry.*

At this moment I had an epiphany/revelation. I tell people it is like the animated characters in a cartoon when they get an idea and the lightbulb comes on over their head. This is exactly what happened to me. I had wondered what I had done that was allowing the onslaught of the devil against me and my family. I had searched everything and repented of anything I could think of. It was all still going on and seemed only to be getting worse. However, here it was being said there was a covenant with a demon power in my ancestry that was allowing me to be sucked dry. These people of course knew nothing about my ongoing situation. They were only announcing what was being perceived in the spirit world. However, I knew immediately that something of great significance was potentially being unveiled. I was going to find later, as I delved into the undoing of these devilish covenants, that where they were in place it gave the devil legal rights to claim me and my lineage. Hence the trouble and decision-making of our children.

In response to this revelation, the people leading this session told me to pray this prayer after them. They were about to help me undo the covenant claims of the devil that were bringing such destruction into my life. They had me pray a prayer of this nature.

> Lord, as I stand before You, I repent for any and all agreement I or my bloodline has with this demon god, Parax. I remind You that I am in covenant with You by the blood of Jesus. Whoever or why this covenant was made, I renounce and repent of it. I ask that according to Hebrews 12:24 the

> blood of sprinkling would speak better things than that of Abel for me. I ask that on the basis of Your blood's voice, every claim of covenant rights by the devil against me would now be revoked and annulled.
>
> In addition, Lord, I also give back anything and everything the devil claims I have gained through this covenant. I want nothing that would come from him. I only want what is mine through my covenant with You and what You have and will provide. In Jesus' Name, amen!

There are things we will discuss in the next chapter that will help some of this make more sense. At the moment you, like me, may have questions concerning what I had just prayed. I was going to learn later that I had been standing in the Courts of Heaven and was undoing the covenant claims the devil had used to harass my life and destiny. I was about to find out, however, that this prayer session of less than 30 minutes was going to be used by God to change the course of my life. Delays, attacks, and hindrances were about to vanish because the legal claims of the devil to hold me in them had now been removed! I was to begin a new journey toward the prophetic promises of God for my life!

CHAPTER 5

WHY NOW?

My life did indeed change. In a very quick fashion it became apparent that whatever had been working against us was gone. We saw the attacks and troubles vanish. We also entered a time of restoration of what had been lost. Influence started to come and even wealth and prosperity began to arrive on a new level. Of course, I knew this was happening because a covenant right the devil had been claiming was removed. I was to discover some issues concerning this as I started to investigate these ideas.

The first thing I wanted to know was why the devil suddenly started to exploit this covenant with this demon god Parax if it had always been there. My life had been blessed of God. Mary and I and our family had lived under the grace of God's favor. Yet all of a sudden these attacks started to come that I couldn't explain. This is what I now believe. I had been a local pastor in one fashion or form for 22 years. I had fought many battles and had won. However, when I stepped out at the word of the Lord to travel and have a larger kingdom impact, I became a bigger threat. In fact, I believe that the devil many times knows what we are meant for before we do. Psalm 139:16 tells us that our destiny, future, and purpose for being alive on the planet was planned in the eternities.

Your eyes saw my substance, being yet unformed.
And in Your book they all were written,
The days fashioned for me,
When as yet there were none of them.

This scripture tells us that before we ever existed in the earth we were planned and our purpose was written down in God's book. This means we have a book in heaven that we are here in the earth to fulfill. In fact, Daniel 7:9-10, in unveiling the Court system of heaven, shows that the Court of Heaven cannot operate without books being opened.

I watched till thrones were put in place,
And the Ancient of Days was seated;
His garment was white as snow,
And the hair of His head was like pure wool.
His throne was a fiery flame,
Its wheels a burning fire;
A fiery stream issued
And came forth from before Him.
A thousand thousands ministered to Him;
Ten thousand times ten thousand stood before Him.
The court was seated,
And the books were opened.

Not all "books" in heaven are opened. Some are shut. Remember that John the apostle wept because of closed books in Revelation 5:1-4.

And I saw in the right hand of Him who sat on the throne a scroll written inside and on the back, sealed with seven seals. Then I saw a strong angel proclaiming with a loud

> *voice, "Who is worthy to open the scroll and to loose its seals?" And no one in heaven or on the earth or under the earth was able to open the scroll, or to look at it.*
>
> *So I wept much, because no one was found worthy to open and read the scroll, or to look at it.*

As long as this book was closed, the purpose and intent of God could not be done. There had to be an opening of this book for the righteous judgments of God to be released. If you investigated closely, you would find that it was Jesus' atoning work and the intercession of John that caused the books to be open. Our intercession is used of God to pray into reality all that Jesus died for. Even our own destiny written and contained in the books of heaven must be opened. This can require our own prayer and intercession. As we passionately seek to know what is in our books, they will open. The result will be revelation that we begin to have of why we are here in the earth.

I remember the day in prayer when suddenly, without prior awareness, the Lord said to me, "You will disciple nations." I knew instantly this was the voice of the Lord. I now know this word came as a result of what is written in my book in heaven. I was made and given the purpose to disciple nations. I also now know in hindsight that this word involved the "Courts of Heaven" teaching. I had been given this revelation and understanding to steward and declare to the nations. God would open massive doors and opportunities for this to be done.

This very thing also happened to Isaiah in Isaiah 6:8-10. Isaiah is having an encounter in the glory of the Lord. He has been made aware of his uncleanness, sin, and iniquity. The seraphim have purged his lips with a coal from the altar of heaven. Now,

Isaiah's ears are opened and he hears God and the council of heaven speaking.

> *Also I heard the voice of the Lord, saying:*
> *"Whom shall I send,*
> *And who will go for Us?"*
>
> *Then I said, "Here am I! Send me."*
>
> *And He said, "Go, and tell this people:*
> *'Keep on hearing, but do not understand;*
> *Keep on seeing, but do not perceive.'*
>
> *"Make the heart of this people dull,*
> *And their ears heavy,*
> *And shut their eyes;*
> *Lest they see with their eyes,*
> *And hear with their ears,*
> *And understand with their heart,*
> *And return and be healed."*

My main point is that Isaiah was chosen from the council of the Lord as the messenger of God. He also was given the message he would carry. I have always had a sense of this as well. God sovereignly chose me to carry and herald the message of the Courts of Heaven. Even though there are others who have picked it up, it primarily originated with me. I don't say this arrogantly. In fact, it is a very humbling and serious matter. I must endeavor to speak of this concept and keep it as pure as I can. I will stand and give an account of my faithfulness in these areas. Less you should think this is boastful, the apostle Paul spoke very similarly in Romans 2:16.

> *In the day when God will judge the secrets of men by Jesus Christ, according to my gospel.*

Wow! What arrogance, we might say. Of course, this isn't so. The apostle Paul knew God had unlocked through him justification through faith. The revelation he had received from God is still changing lives today. He called this gospel "my gospel." He had the audacity to say that judgment would be rendered into people's lives according to the revelation he had dispensed. He spoke of *my gospel* in other places as well. Second Timothy 2:8 proclaims that Paul's gospel declared Jesus was raised from the dead.

> *Remember that Jesus Christ, of the seed of David, was raised from the dead according to my gospel.*

Paul felt so strongly about the stewardship of the gospel that he again called it *my gospel.* This strongly implies that God had committed something to Paul to make sure it is heralded correctly. There are several other scriptures that speak of Paul's awareness of making sure the gospel was properly managed. First Timothy 1:9-11 gives a clear depiction from Paul of his certainty of the gospel being under his care.

> *Knowing this: that the law is not made for a righteous person, but for the lawless and insubordinate, for the ungodly and for sinners, for the unholy and profane, for murderers of fathers and murderers of mothers, for manslayers, for fornicators, for sodomites, for kidnappers, for liars, for perjurers, and if there is any other thing that is contrary to sound doctrine, according to the glorious gospel of the blessed God which was committed to my trust.*

Paul is letting it be known that the basis of sound doctrine is the glorious gospel he has been entrusted with. This is why he is so aggressive in protecting this from impurity and pollution.

I actually feel the same way about the Courts of Heaven message. This message by its very nature can become fodder for those who are not biblically based. They can began to let their *experience* dictate doctrine. However, I am a strong proponent that anything and everything we teach must be backed up by the word of God. Otherwise, we can began to slip away into deception. It is good and fine to have experiences in God. But we must be able to line it up with the word of God. This will keep us on the right track and accountable to God and others.

When the Lord from His council decided to make me His messenger concerning the Courts of Heaven, the devil commissioned a seeking out of a legal right to destroy me. It would be similar to a prosecuting attorney hiring a private investigator to discover issues from our past. Once these issues are uncovered, he can now use them against us. No one is going to go to that trouble unless you have become a threat to their intent. This is why for decades the whole idea of there being in covenant with a demon-god named Parax had no bearing on my life. As long as I was a local pastor with limited influence, I was of little threat. However, when I began to have a global effect, there was a need to stop me. This is when satan and his forces commissioned a seeking of my history and ancestry to discover anything legal that would allow them to consume me. This is when the covenant and agreement with Parax was discovered. All of a sudden, attacks and destruction began to come into our lives. This is the first secret you should know concerning undoing covenants with demons. This sometimes helps answer *why* something is happening out of the blue. First Peter 4:12-13 tells us we are not to think it strange when difficult times arise.

Beloved, do not think it strange concerning the fiery trial which is to try you, as though some strange thing happened to you; but rejoice to the extent that you partake of Christ's sufferings, that when His glory is revealed, you may also be glad with exceeding joy.

We are told here that we shouldn't think it out of the ordinary if trouble comes to us. We should make sure that any suffering is for the glory of God. However, we must also know that the devil can only bring destruction to us, if he has found a legal right in us or our bloodline. First Peter 5:8 lets us know that the devil is our legal opponent and is looking for a legal right to devour us.

Be sober, be vigilant; because your adversary the devil walks about like a roaring lion, seeking whom he may devour.

The word *adversary* in the Greek is *antidikos.* It means "one who brings a lawsuit." The devil cannot just decide to devour and consume us. He must have a legal right to do it. He searches for this right. This is why the devil is spoken of several times as walking about or going to and fro. We see this phrase used when God asked the devil where he had been in Job 1:7-8.

And the Lord said to Satan, "From where do you come?"

So Satan answered the Lord and said, "From going to and fro on the earth, and from walking back and forth on it."

Then the Lord said to Satan, "Have you considered My servant Job, that there is none like him on the earth, a

> *blameless and upright man, one who fears God and shuns evil?"*

When satan admitted to God that he had been going to and fro and back and forth, the Lord then asked him about Job. This is because the phrase satan used describes someone searching and seeking things out. God was asking satan if he had *found* anything in Job. We, of course, know the end result of this. Satan accused not only Job but God of inordinately setting a divine protection around Job. God allowed the protection to be removed and satan to touch Job. Based on the case against Job and actually God Himself, satan brought destructive things to Job and his family. The result was tribulation and struggles for Job, but ultimately victory, redemption, and vindication. It was a navigation in the Courts of Heaven for Job that allowed this end to be accomplished. In the process, God dealt with issues in Job's life but brought him through as one of His chosen ones. The Lord will do the same for us as we maneuver in the Courts of Heaven and see judgments set in place for us.

> As I come into Your Courts, Lord, I thank You for the kingdom purpose You have set for me. I am so honored to be a part of Your will in the earth. However, any legal claim the devil has against me to prohibit this, I ask for a judgment against it and him. May it be known before Your Courts that this is about Your will, purpose, and intent in the earth. Therefore arise, O God, and bring verdicts against the powers of satan. Let their will not be done, but Yours. May You find in me a humble servant desiring to complete all You ordained from the books of heaven. In Jesus' Name, amen.

CHAPTER 6

UNDOING CREATED COVENANTS

A second key/secret to undoing covenants with demons is to realize why they might exist. In Isaiah 28:14-15 we see God's people making covenant with devilish powers. They clearly are in a backslidden state.

> *Therefore hear the word of the Lord, you scornful men,*
> *Who rule this people who are in Jerusalem,*
> *Because you have said, "We have made a covenant with death,*
> *And with Sheol we are in agreement.*
> *When the overflowing scourge passes through,*
> *It will not come to us,*
> *For we have made lies our refuge,*
> *And under falsehood we have hidden ourselves."*

These leaders of Israel made agreement with Sheol. This is a term that implies joining themselves in union with devilish powers. Notice that the reason they make this covenant with devils is for protection against disaster and attack. Our ancestors might have made covenants with supernatural demonic powers for this purpose. They could have made covenant for the intent of rain for their harvest. They could have made covenant for someone sick to be healed. They could have made covenant to live with "blessing" and "favor" on their life. It could have been for any number of reasons. If they acknowledged these powers of darkness and agreed with them through offerings, these powers will not let go until they are required to. If we are to fully understand this, we must recognize how covenants come into place. Covenants with demons can occur intentionally or unintentionally. The intentional covenants are a result of *trades resulting in covenants that produce dedications.* Trades are offerings that declare a covenant entered into. We see this when Abraham gave Abimelech seven ewe lambs in Genesis 21:27-32. There had been disputes over who owned wells that had been dug. Abraham ended this dispute through making a covenant through a trade.

> *So Abraham took sheep and oxen and gave them to Abimelech, and the two of them made a covenant. And Abraham set seven ewe lambs of the flock by themselves.*
>
> *Then Abimelech asked Abraham, "What is the meaning of these seven ewe lambs which you have set by themselves?"*
>
> *And he said, "You will take these seven ewe lambs from my hand, that they may be my witness that I have dug this well." Therefore he called that place Beersheba, because the two of them swore an oath there.*
>
> *Thus they made a covenant at Beersheba. So Abimelech rose with Phichol, the commander of his army, and they returned to the land of the Philistines.*

Trades produce covenants. The devil understands this, because this is how he operated even in heaven. Ezekiel 28:14-16 shows that the devil sought to use trades to get what he wanted. His trades became polluted because of the iniquity in his heart. In other words, they were of a wrong motive.

> *You were the anointed cherub who covers;*
> *I established you;*
> *You were on the holy mountain of God;*
> *You walked back and forth in the midst of fiery stones.*
> *You were perfect in your ways from the day you were created,*
> *Till iniquity was found in you.*
>
> *By the abundance of your trading*
> *You became filled with violence within,*
> *And you sinned;*
> *Therefore I cast you as a profane thing*
> *Out of the mountain of God;*
> *And I destroyed you, O covering cherub,*
> *From the midst of the fiery stones.*

Before satan was God's archenemy in the earth, he was an anointed cherub in heaven. His heavenly function was *trading*. There was nothing wrong with trading. This is what satan did as lucifer, while he was in heaven. It was only after iniquity was found in his heart that his trading became polluted. We must understand that *trading* is a heavenly and spiritual activity. Trading is what Jesus did on the cross for us. He made a trade for us that secured our redemption. Second Corinthians 5:21 tells us that we are made His righteousness because of a trade.

For He made Him who knew no sin to be sin for us, that we might become the righteousness of God in Him.

He became our sin that we might become His righteousness. This was a trade. Again, trading is a spiritual/heavenly activity.

We also see a trade in what Jesus did on the cross to secure our healing. Isaiah 53:4 lets us know that Jesus traded so that we could be healed.

Surely He has borne our griefs
And carried our sorrows;
Yet we esteemed Him stricken,
Smitten by God, and afflicted.

The word *griefs* in the Hebrew literally means "maladies, sicknesses, and diseases." The word *sorrows* means "pains." When Jesus suffered and died on the cross, He took pain, sickness, and disease on Himself and gave us health and wholeness. When we get healed, we are entering into His trade for us!

We also see that poverty's legal right to control us and determine our future was ruined and broken. Second Corinthians 8:9 lets us know that Jesus, in a trade on the cross, gave us the right to be rich while He took our poverty!

For you know the grace of our Lord Jesus Christ, that though He was rich, yet for your sakes He became poor, that you through His poverty might become rich.

Clearly we see that Jesus traded away His riches so that poverty would be broken from us. This allows us to be rich. When the Bible says Jesus was rich, that is not speaking of His heavenly wealth before He came to the earth. It is speaking of His economic status while in the earth. The spirit of religion wants to make us think Jesus was poor. This spirit uses Matthew 8:19-20 to seek to make us think as believers we are *supposed* to be poor.

> *Then a certain scribe came and said to Him, "Teacher, I will follow You wherever You go."*
>
> *And Jesus said to him, "Foxes have holes and birds of the air have nests, but the Son of Man has nowhere to lay His head."*

This spirit of religion and those under its influence use this scripture to say Jesus was so poor, He had nowhere to even sleep. This scripture is not speaking of this. Jesus said this in reference to His lifestyle of travel, ministry, and evangelism. He was pointing out the rigors of ministry if this scribe was going to become one of His followers. Jesus wanted him to know what he was signing up for. However, Jesus was not poor in His earthly life. Let me give you some insight to back this up!

First of all, the wise men or magi who came to worship Him from the east were men of great wealth. They brought expensive gifts to worship Him with. Matthew 2:11 shows us the expensive gifts these men brought to Jesus. They knew by revelation who He was.

> *And when they had come into the house, they saw the young Child with Mary His mother, and fell down and worshiped Him. And when they had opened their treasures, they presented gifts to Him: gold, frankincense, and myrrh.*

The word *treasure* in the Greek is the word *thesauros.* It means "a deposit, wealth." Notice that these wealthy men gave to Jesus gold, frankincense, and myrrh. As they opened their treasures, they worshiped Him with great riches and wealth. These gifts they brought could have been in today's wealth equivalent to $4 million. This is what some believe. According to an article in the *Williamsport-Sun Gazette*:

> According to medieval legend, the names of the three Wise Men were Melchior, King of Arabia (gold); Gaspar, King of Tarsus (myrrh) and Balthasar, King of Ethiopia (frankincense). These three names have neither appeared in the Bible nor in Christian literature until 500 years after the birth of Jesus. Scholars cannot agree on the names of the three men nor from where they traveled. However, it is agreed three gifts were brought.
>
> The gifts, which the three men carried, were fit for a King. Equivalent to today's prices, a pound of frankincense was worth $500 a pound, and a pound of myrrh was $4,000. Today, each are priced at approximately $15 a pound. However, the value of a pound of gold was valued at $600, and in today's market, a pound of gold could cost 10 times that amount.[1]
>
> The Magi gifts were of great value, with some estimating the value of these items around $4 million by our standards. How much of the gold, frankincense and myrrh were given we are not told. We don't really know how many wise men came to see the Child.[2]

Wow! In today's worth, $4 million was potentially brought to worship Jesus. Others have valued these gifts at much more. This means that Mary and Joseph and Jesus, regardless of their economic status before this, were instantly wealthy and rich.

Jesus also had a house in Capernaum, it appears. Matthew 4:12-16 says that Jesus *dwelt* in this place to fulfill a prophetic word.

> *Now when Jesus heard that John had been put in prison, He departed to Galilee. And leaving Nazareth, He came and dwelt in Capernaum, which is by the sea, in the regions of Zebulun and Naphtali, that it might be fulfilled which was spoken by Isaiah the prophet, saying:*
>
> *"The land of Zebulun and the land of Naphtali,*
> *By the way of the sea, beyond the Jordan,*
> *Galilee of the Gentiles:*
> *The people who sat in darkness have seen a great light,*
> *And upon those who sat in the region and shadow of death*
> *Light has dawned."*

The word *dwelt* in the Greek is *katoikeo.* It means "to house permanently, reside, inhabitant." This has every indication that Jesus owned this house in Capernaum. Jesus' presence in this place released a light and impact in this area. It was something that the prophet Isaiah had prophesied centuries before. The Bible speaks several times about Jesus coming to Capernaum and being in the *house.* This is because this was *His own house.*

Mark 2:1 relates the infamous account of the roof being dismantled to get a man into the presence of Jesus. This reference speaks of Jesus being in the house in Capernaum.

> *And again He entered Capernaum after some days, and it was heard that He was in the house.*

Mark 9:33-34 shows Jesus returning to this house with His disciples. In this setting, He began to ask them what they argued about on the way there.

> *Then He came to Capernaum. And when He was in the house He asked them, "What was it you disputed among yourselves on the road?" But they kept silent, for on the road they had disputed among themselves who would be the greatest.*

Jesus would return to this house in Capernaum because it was His house. He was not poor and homeless. He had a place to return to from His ministry trips. It seems to be a place where He would come to with His disciples.

Another thing that attests to Jesus' wealth was His robe was very expensive. John 19:23-24 shows that Jesus' robe was so expensive that the soldiers didn't want to destroy it.

> *Then the soldiers, when they had crucified Jesus, took His garments and made four parts, to each soldier a part, and also the tunic. Now the tunic was without seam, woven from the top in one piece. They said therefore among themselves, "Let us not tear it, but cast lots for it, whose it shall be," that the Scripture might be fulfilled which says:*
>
> *"They divided My garments among them,*
> *And for My clothing they cast lots."*

Therefore the soldiers did these things.

Jesus and His ministry were wealthy enough to take care of 12 men and their families while they traveled and ministered. Remember that these men left everything to follow Jesus. Luke 5:11 says they left everything to become disciples of Jesus.

> *So when they had brought their boats to land, they forsook all and followed Him.*

Mark 1:17-18 shows Peter and Andrew forsaking their livelihood to follow Jesus:

> *Then Jesus said to them, "Follow Me, and I will make you become fishers of men." They immediately left their nets and followed Him.*

This means that as they traveled and ministered, the men and their families were cared for financially by Jesus. Luke 9:11-13 shows that Jesus told His disciples to feed the multitude. We know that He is about to multiply the fishes and loaves. However, notice that the disciples speak of going and buying food for all these thousands.

> *But when the multitudes knew it, they followed Him; and He received them and spoke to them about the kingdom of God, and healed those who had need of healing. When the day began to wear away, the twelve came and said to Him, "Send the multitude away, that they may go into the surrounding towns and country, and lodge and get provisions; for we are in a deserted place here."*
>
> *But He said to them, "You give them something to eat."*

> *And they said, "We have no more than five loaves and two fish, unless we go and buy food for all these people."*

The disciples acknowledged that they had enough money to buy food for thousands of people. This is because Jesus and His ministry were rich. There was no lack or need among them.

A final thought I would bring to verify Jesus' earthly wealth was that even though Judas stole money from the money bag, there was still plenty. John 12:6 declares that Judas was a thief and took some of what was in the money box.

> *This he said, not that he cared for the poor, but because he was a thief, and had the money box; and he used to take what was put in it.*

Even though Judas stole, there was clearly still plenty for the disciples to live and minister from.

All of this and more testify to Jesus' earthly wealth. So when the Bible says that He became poor though He was rich, it is speaking of a trade He made for us. His allowing of this judged the poverty spirit that wants to hold us in poverty. His trade for us allows us to prosper and even become rich!

I have pointed this out to let us know that *trading* is heavenly/spiritual activity. Lucifer in his heavenly dimension *traded* for God's purposes to be done. However, when iniquity entered him, his trading began to flow from impure motives and evil agendas. He began to operate in this powerful principle to ascend above God. Isaiah 14:12-15 gives us insight into what was in his heart.

> *How you are fallen from heaven,*
> *O Lucifer, son of the morning!*

How you are cut down to the ground,
You who weakened the nations!
For you have said in your heart:
"I will ascend into heaven,
I will exalt my throne above the stars of God;
I will also sit on the mount of the congregation
On the farthest sides of the north;
I will ascend above the heights of the clouds,
I will be like the Most High."
Yet you shall be brought down to Sheol,
To the lowest depths of the Pit.

Trading is so powerful that it would have allowed lucifer to accomplish this. God did not just cast him out of the heavenly realm because He was angry with him. He knew if He allowed him to stay in this dimension and function there, he would accomplish his evil purpose. Therefore, according to scripture God cast him out of the holy mountain and off the fiery stones. This was the dimension and place of trading. However, when satan came into the earth, he understood the power of trading. This is why he was able to convince Adam and Eve to trade with him. He offered them sin and they took it. In Genesis 3:4-7, satan convinced them to trade with him.

Then the serpent said to the woman, "You will not surely die. For God knows that in the day you eat of it your eyes will be opened, and you will be like God, knowing good and evil."

So when the woman saw that the tree was good for food, that it was pleasant to the eyes, and a tree desirable to make one wise, she took of its fruit and ate. She also

> *gave to her husband with her, and he ate. Then the eyes of both of them were opened, and they knew that they were naked; and they sewed fig leaves together and made themselves coverings.*

The principle is simply this. When they took what satan offered them in a trade, it gave him the right to take what they had, which was authority over the earth. Any trade those in our bloodline have made with satan will allow him legal grounds to take what is supposed to be ours. However, Jesus undid any and all trades with satan through His own trade for us. We undo the trades we have made with satan through agreeing with the trade of Jesus for us. Anytime we are tempted, it is satan seeking to pull us onto his trading floor. We must repent for any place we have done this and ask for the trade of Jesus to speak for us in the Courts of Heaven. Anyone who has made covenant with demon powers intentionally did so through a trade that created a covenant. This allow the enemy to claim that we and our lineage belong to him. We are dedicated to him through the trade that created the covenant. We must go into the Courts of Heaven and undo the trade, annul the covenant, and revoke any and all dedications to the devil and his power! This can free us from bloodline issues used by the devil against us.

> As I approach Your Courts, Lord, I ask that any trades with the devil that I might have made or that are in my bloodline/ancestry might be undone. May these trades with satanic powers that created covenants be undone by Your trade for us. Thank You so much, Lord, for what You did on the cross for us. Let every trade with satan and his partners that has been made by me or my ancestry

be nullified. In Jesus' Name let it be undone. Let it be recorded and known before the Courts that I repent for any such activity. I also renounce all agreements with darkness. May the work of Jesus on the cross speak for me and revoke every legal agreement through trading. Let me and my lineage go free from any and all demonic influences and harassments. May I come into full places of walking out what is written in the books of heaven about me. In Jesus' Name, amen.

NOTES

1. Bill Bower, "Gifts of Wise Men still used today," *Williamsport-Sun Gazette,* December 22, 2020, https://www.sungazette.com/news/outdoors/2020/12/gifts-of-wise-men-still-used-today.
2. Bruce Kessler, "The gift," The Norman Transcript, December 3, 2021, https://www.normantranscript.com/community/the-gift/article_262e4186-53a2-11ec-9901-37fa58e0bdd3.html.

CHAPTER 7

REPENTANCE

We have looked at a couple of ideas of how covenants with demons originated. They are the result of the devil commissioning a searching of our bloodline because we have become a bigger threat. He is seeking to secure a legal claim against us. This is because he knows that if we aren't stopped we will be a part of his demise. Let me speak to this for just a moment. What is the real motive of the devil to hinder and destroy our future by attacking us? It really isn't because he doesn't want us happy. It is because he is seeking to stay out of hell and his eternal demise. Revelation 12:12 tells us that the devil is aware that his time is running out. He knows that the day will come when he is ultimately judged forever. He is seeking to postpone it for as long as he can.

> *Therefore rejoice, O heavens, and you who dwell in them! Woe to the inhabitants of the earth and the sea! For the devil has come down to you, having great wrath, because he knows that he has a short time.*

The closer satan gets to his total destruction, the more wrath that he will operate in. This is why we see the things happening within the world today. The anger and wrath of satan is fighting and striking out at God and His authority. However, satan is wise enough to know that his judgment isn't a date set on a calendar. It is tied to the purposes of God being done in the earth. If he can hinder God's will from being done in the earth, he can postpone his inevitable judgment. Remember in Hebrews 10:12-13 that Jesus is sitting and *waiting* for His enemies to be made His footstool.

> *But this Man, after He had offered one sacrifice for sins forever, sat down at the right hand of God, from that time waiting till His enemies are made His footstool.*

Who or what is Jesus waiting on? He is waiting on us as the church to finish the job He left us to do. We are to take the authority God granted us and use it to subdue God's enemies under His feet! In other words, if satan can hinder us from getting the job accomplished, his judgment will be postponed indefinitely. The end of all things cannot happen until the church sets into place all that Jesus died for. Then the judgment against the devil can be enacted. This is why we as the church are a huge part of determining the end of all things. Second Peter 3:11-12 tells us clearly that we are what determines *when* Jesus comes back and satan is ultimately judged.

> *Therefore, since all these things will be dissolved, what manner of persons ought you to be in holy conduct and godliness, looking for and hastening the coming of the day of God, because of which the heavens will be dissolved, being on fire, and the elements will melt with fervent heat?*

The word *hastening* is the Greek word *speudo* and it means "to speed up." We are being told that we can *speed up* the timing of Jesus coming back and satan being judged. The devil knows this.

So he is aggressively working to hinder us from getting the job done. This is why he tempts us, seeking to cause us to be distracted and to stumble. It is also why he searched our bloodline for legal rights to resist and hinder us. As mentioned previously, each of us has a destiny written in the books of heaven concerning us. Again, so we can be clear, Psalm 139:15-16 unveils this idea to us. We are here in the earth on assignment as a part of the purposes of God in the earth.

> *My frame was not hidden from You,*
> *When I was made in secret,*
> *And skillfully wrought in the lowest parts of the earth.*
> *Your eyes saw my substance, being yet unformed.*
> *And in Your book they all were written,*
> *The days fashioned for me,*
> *When as yet there were none of them.*

My purpose, intent, and reason for being alive on this planet was written in a book in heaven before time began or existed. We all have this in God. We are here to be a part of God's divine plan. God's plan is not just to give us a wonderful, fulfilling life. It is to use our lives as a part of the fulfillment of His will, so satan can be judged! Ephesians 2:10 lets us know that we are the workmanship of God to fulfill what was ordained for us in eternity past!

> *For we are His workmanship, created in Christ Jesus for good works, which God prepared beforehand that we should walk in them.*

The Lord, as the Master, has pre-ordained us to fulfill a piece of His plan. When each of us does what we were ordained to accomplish, God's ultimate will gets done. This is called the *mystery of God* in Revelation 10:7.

> *But in the days of the sounding of the seventh angel, when he is about to sound, the mystery of God would be finished, as He declared to His servants the prophets.*

The redemptive plan of God to reclaim man and judge the devil is referred to as the *mystery of God.* This is because we don't completely understand it, but it will be fulfilled in finality. The interesting thing is while there is the mystery of God at work in the earth, there is also the *mystery of iniquity or lawlessness* working. Second Thessalonians 2:7 says this mystery is also at work today.

> *For the mystery of lawlessness is already at work; only He who now restrains will do so until He is taken out of the way.*

This mystery's purpose is to disrupt and interrupt the intentions of God, i.e., the mystery of God. This is because satan is trying to stay out of the pit of hell. The way he seeks to do this is through stopping each of us from fulfilling the destiny we were created for. He uses the power of iniquity/lawlessness to accomplish this. It is interesting that there is a mystery attached to iniquity/lawlessness. This is what greatly empowers the demonic purposes against the purposes of God. When we deal with iniquity, we are undoing that which satan uses to defer the will of God in the earth. The word *iniquity/lawlessness* in the Hebrew is the word *anomia.* It means "illegality, a violation of law." Satan is using that which is *illegal.* As we deal with the legal claims of iniquity, we are stopping the mystery of iniquity/lawlessness from working against the purposes of God. Our destinies fulfilled will bring to pass the purposes of God in the earth, which is the mystery of God!

If satan can stop and interrupt this, then he will stop his judgment from occurring indefinitely. He knows it will happen; he is seeking to postpone it as long as he can. This is why he works against us. This is why he searches our bloodlines to discover legal rights to hinder us in our destiny. If he can accomplish this, he can through desperation keep himself free. The moment we learn how to remove the legal claims against us and get our destiny, we have just brought a great strike against the powers of darkness and their intent.

With all this said, another significant piece of annulling bloodline issues is repentance. Repentance for ourselves and our bloodlines is essential to revoking legal claims against us. When we repent and ask for the blood of sprinkling to speak for us, legal claims against us are removed. Repentance allows us to recover ourselves from the powers of darkness according to 2 Timothy 2:24-26.

> *And a servant of the Lord must not quarrel but be gentle to all, able to teach, patient, in humility correcting those who are in opposition, if God perhaps will grant them repentance, so that they may know the truth, and that they may come to their senses and escape the snare of the devil, having been taken captive by him to do his will.*

The devil desires to ensnare us and take us captive to do his will. However, when God grants us repentance we can come free from this snare. The phrase *come to their senses* actually means to *become sober again*. This is what happened to the prodigal son Jesus told the story about in Luke 15:17-18. We are told that he *came to himself* while he was in the pig pen.

> *But when he came to himself, he said, "How many of my father's hired servants have bread enough and to spare, and I perish with hunger! I will arise and go to my father, and will say to him, 'Father, I have sinned against heaven and before you.'"*

Notice that when he came to himself and realized the condition he was in, he decided to go home to his father. Real repentance always involves a *decision* being made. This is because repentance is a changing of the mind. The Greek word for *repentance* is *metanoia.* It doesn't just mean a changing of direction. There must first be a changing of the mind. This is what happened to the prodigal son and brought him home. It is also what Paul told Timothy has to happen to get free from the snares of the devil that he has trapped us in. Notice, too, that this is repentance that God has to grant. In other words, we don't just decide to repent; God has to grant it to us out of His grace and kindness.

This is true on a personal level but also when repenting for bloodline issues. I remember when I began to repent for covenants with demons in my bloodline, the sorrow and emotional pain I felt. This was because God was *granting* me repentance. This is what Paul spoke of in 2 Corinthians 7:9-10. There are two kinds of sorrow that Paul is speaking of here. There is godly sorrow and worldly sorrow. One brings repentance to life, the other brings death.

> *Now I rejoice, not that you were made sorry, but that your sorrow led to repentance. For you were made sorry in a godly manner, that you might suffer loss from us in*

> *nothing. For godly sorrow produces repentance leading to salvation, not to be regretted; but the sorrow of the world produces death.*

Notice that the godly sorrow causes us not to suffer any kind of loss. This principle is unveiled in two of Jesus' early disciples. Peter is an example of godly sorrow, while Judas is an example of worldly sorrow. Of course both of these were disciples of the Lord, yet they responded completely differently. Both of these failed Jesus on immense levels. Peter denied the Lord three times before the rooster crowed. This was what Jesus had said he would do. As morning was dawning, Peter denied that he knew the Lord. In Luke 22:55-62 as the rooster crowed, Peter's denial is made even as Jesus had said.

> *Now when they had kindled a fire in the midst of the courtyard and sat down together, Peter sat among them. And a certain servant girl, seeing him as he sat by the fire, looked intently at him and said, "This man was also with Him."*
>
> *But he denied Him, saying, "Woman, I do not know Him."*
>
> *And after a little while another saw him and said, "You also are of them."*
>
> *But Peter said, "Man, I am not!"*
>
> *Then after about an hour had passed, another confidently affirmed, saying, "Surely this fellow also was with Him, for he is a Galilean."*
>
> *But Peter said, "Man, I do not know what you are saying!"*

> *Immediately, while he was still speaking, the rooster crowed. And the Lord turned and looked at Peter. Then Peter remembered the word of the Lord, how He had said to him, "Before the rooster crows, you will deny Me three times." So Peter went out and wept bitterly.*

The weeping of Peter was a part of the repentance that he went through. He was coming to the realization of the weakness of his own flesh. He was recognizing that there was no power in himself to serve the Lord. He could want to, but he needed the empowerment of the Lord. This is exactly what he received on the Day of Pentecost when the Spirit came. Yet the process involved deep levels of godly sorrow that produced repentance unto life.

Judas on the other hand had worldly sorrow. Remember that he betrayed the Lord but then came to a place of remorse. However, remorse is not necessarily repentance. In Matthew 27:3-5, we see Judas bringing back the 30 pieces of silver that were paid him to betray Jesus. He threw them down and went out and hanged himself.

> *Then Judas, His betrayer, seeing that He had been condemned, was remorseful and brought back the thirty pieces of silver to the chief priests and elders, saying, "I have sinned by betraying innocent blood."*
>
> *And they said, "What is that to us? You see to it!"*
>
> *Then he threw down the pieces of silver in the temple and departed, and went and hanged himself.*

We know that Judas was suffering from worldly sorrow and not godly sorrow. This is because godly sorrow will bring us to hope for our future. Judas had no hope and as a result hanged himself.

I believe that if Judas had really repented, he would have been restored. The problem was, there was no real repentance. The word that is translated *remorseful* is the Greek word *metamellonai.* It means to "regret or care afterward." It appears Judas was sorry for what he had caused but had no real care about the purposes of God. Sometimes our repentance is more a sorrow connected to the consequences of our sin rather than the effect on God's heart. I believe real repentance feels pain for what we did to God. It's more than a pain concerning what I might suffer. Only the Spirit of the Lord can bring me to this place of repentance. This is why we must be granted repentance. The bottom line is that clearly Judas was in worldly sorrow or he wouldn't have hanged himself. This is not to say that God granted Peter repentance and not Judas. Peter's heart was in a yielded posture before the Lord; Judas' wasn't. Even though God grants repentance, the state of our hearts is an essential part of the equation. Through our seeking of God and passion for Him, we become sensitive to His heart. Otherwise we can become hardened and indifferent to the drawing of the Lord to repentance. True repentance will bring us to hope for our future. It will lead us to life. Let's ask the Holy Spirit to do the necessary work in our hearts that we might experience godly sorrow and not worldly sorrow.

This godly sorrow that leads to real repentance recovers anything and everything the devil has stolen. This is because this level of repentance revokes legal claims of the devil against us. This is not just words in our mouth but deep levels of emotional recognition that bring real change. This level of repentance speaks greatly in the Courts of Heaven. This is why as I repented of covenants with demons, I could *feel* this deep emotional stirring of sorrow in my heart. This was not natural; this was supernatural. This is what I believe 1 John 1:9 is speaking about.

> *If we confess our sins, He is faithful and just to forgive us our sins and to cleanse us from all unrighteousness.*

Notice that there are two separate things that happen at the confession of our sins. There is the forgiveness of sins and also the cleansing of all unrighteousness. Forgiveness of sin is the legal response of God to our confession. Our confession grants God the legal right to forgive our sins personally and in our bloodline. This stops the devil from using these sins against us as legal fodder.

The word *confession* is the Greek word *homologeo.* It means "to say the same thing, or to agree." In other words, real confession of sin is when we say the same thing about our sin that God says about it. This is very powerful. This is when God can *legally* forgive us of our sin and the devil has no right to steal from us because of our sin. *Homologeo* is the granting of authority by an official authority. This may be a court of law, a government department, or an academic or professional body. Our agreement with God through confession is our testimony that allows Him as Judge to forgive our sin. This is why our confession concerning bloodline issues deals with legal claims of the devil against us.

Notice also that in addition to our confession allowing legal forgiveness, it also releases a cleansing. It is one thing to be forgiven our sins; it is another to have the defilement of our sins washed away. Sin in our lives or our bloodline has a defiling effect on us. It alters our perception of ourselves and gives us a sense of unworthiness and condemnation. When there is a cleansing of unrighteousness from our lives, this is erased and eradicated. If we do not experience this second result of confession, the defilement of sin will pull us back into it. This is what is being spoken of in Hebrews 10:22. There is a cleansing of our conscience from the defilement of sin.

This allows not just us to be forgiven, but also the washing and cleansing away of every defilement.

> *Let us draw near with a true heart in full assurance of faith, having our hearts sprinkled from an evil conscience and our bodies washed with pure water.*

This is what occurs when we draw near to God and into His manifest presence. Our hearts become sprinkled from an evil conscience. All the guilt, condemnation, sense of unworthiness, and fear of judgment is washed away. We are functionally made new. This is what should occur when we confess and agree with God's testimony about our sin. The legal rights of sin are revoked. There will be no loss because of our sin or that in our bloodline. This is because the washing away of the defilement is through the power of the Holy Spirit. The Holy Spirit comes as our *parakletos,* which is the Greek word for *helper* found in John 14:16-17.

> *And I will pray the Father, and He will give you another Helper, that He may abide with you forever—the Spirit of truth, whom the world cannot receive, because it neither sees Him nor knows Him; but you know Him, for He dwells with you and will be in you.*

This word *Helper or Parakletos* means a "legal aid." The Holy Spirit, as our legal aid, helps us make cases in the Courts of Heaven, but He also helps execute the full verdict of the cross into place. This is on our behalf, so that we get the full benefit of all Jesus died for us to have. With regard to our redemption, the Holy Spirit takes the legal work of the cross and brings the full benefits into our lives. This is where not only are we forgiven, but we are cleansed from every defilement of the flesh. The sense of all uncleanness is washed away. We become new and fresh in Him. This is all a result of a confession that is a part of our true repentance.

If we are to fully appreciate the power of repentance, we must understand the testimony of the blood of sprinkling. We are told in Hebrews 12:24 that we have come to *the blood of sprinkling speaking better things.*

> *To Jesus the Mediator of the new covenant, and to the blood of sprinkling that speaks better things than that of Abel.*

If we read the whole discourse of Hebrews 12:22-24, we find it describing the spiritual dimension we have been transferred into. This is why it declares *we have come to.* In other words, we has been translated into a new realm of spiritual positioning. This is by virtue of our new birth. Part of what we have *come to* is the blood of Jesus that is speaking better things than that of Abel. When we examine the life of Abel, of course we find that he brought a great offering to God. His brother Cain, on the other hand, brought an insufficient offering that God rejected. This eventually resulted in Cain arising in envy and killing Abel. Abel's blood, according to Genesis 4:9-12, cried out from the ground.

> *Then the Lord said to Cain, "Where is Abel your brother?"*
>
> *He said, "I do not know. Am I my brother's keeper?"*
>
> *And He said, "What have you done? The voice of your brother's blood cries out to Me from the ground. So now you are cursed from the earth, which has opened its mouth to receive your brother's blood from your hand. When*

> *you till the ground, it shall no longer yield its strength to you. A fugitive and a vagabond you shall be on the earth."*

The cry of Abel's blood was one of vindication, judgment, and retribution. It gave testimony that demanded God judge Cain. On the basis of the testimony of Abel's blood, Cain was judged and sentenced. When the Bible says there is a blood of sprinkling speaking better things than that of Abel, it is clearly talking of Jesus' blood. Whereas Abel's blood testified for judgment, Jesus' blood is crying for forgiveness, redemption, restoration, and reconciliation. The truth is that God has always had a desire to forgive, He just didn't have the legal right to do it until Jesus' blood was shed. This is why we are told that all the Old Testament sacrifices could not fully atone for our sin. Hebrews 10:1-4 gives us understanding that all the sacrifices previous to Jesus' death on the cross were not able to remove sin. They could only roll the sin away for a year at a time. The only thing that could totally and sufficiently remove the legal complaint of sin was Jesus' blood.

> *For the law, having a shadow of the good things to come, and not the very image of the things, can never with these same sacrifices, which they offer continually year by year, make those who approach perfect. For then would they not have ceased to be offered? For the worshipers, once purified, would have had no more consciousness of sins. But in those sacrifices there is a reminder of sins every year. For it is not possible that the blood of bulls and goats could take away sins.*

The offerings mandated by the law were simply a shadow of the ultimate offering of Jesus. Therefore, when they were operated in, they were unable to remove the effects of sin permanently. They could only legally have an effect temporarily. However, when Jesus offered Himself and His blood, this was the legal statement God needed to forgive sins forever. No longer were they rolled off for a year, only to be remembered again. They were completely and totally removed once and for all. Through the blood of Jesus, the legal mandate needed by God to forgive sins forever was satisfied.

With this said, it is repentance that sets us in agreement with the speaking blood. We are told in 1 John 1:7 that when we functionally walk with Jesus, the blood operates for us. We get the benefit of all that Jesus has done for us.

> *But if we walk in the light as He is in the light, we have fellowship with one another, and the blood of Jesus Christ His Son cleanses us from all sin.*

Walking in the light as He is in the light means we are not walking in sin or practicing it in rebellion. This doesn't mean we are perfect and never sin. It does mean that if we do sin, we acknowledge and repent of it quickly. I remember years ago, as a young minister on staff in the church where I was raised up, going to my pastor and confessing my sin. I had in those days rented a movie that had unclean things in it. I had watched it and felt so condemned about the defilement that was in my spirit. I had repented in the privacy of my own life. However, as I repented, I felt I heard the Lord tell me to bring my sin to light. I understood that I was to go confess my sin to my pastor. This is according to James 5:16.

> *Confess your trespasses to one another, and pray for one another, that you may be healed. The effective, fervent prayer of a righteous man avails much.*

I believe that dealing with sin and having a willingness to confess it can bring new effectiveness in prayer. This is why this verse connects these two issues. When I, in certain circumstances, confess my sin to someone else, healing on every level can be released. This is because the legal rights of the devil are unlocked and removed from us. Plus I can move into a new place of effective and fervent prayer as the righteous.

As I went to my pastor to confess this sin that seemed so grievous to me, I honestly thought there was a strong likelihood that I would be fired. I imagined that he would say to me that he appreciated my honesty and repentance, but I couldn't be associate pastor and live this way. I went into his office with fear and trembling. I stood before his desk and he sat behind it. I said, "Brother James, I need to tell you something." With fear in my heart and tears streaming down my face, I confessed to him what I had done. I remember that in the moment I probably wasn't very coherent and clear. I was crying and even sobbing. It was a mixture of deep repentance, but also fear that I was about to lose my job.

Someone might ask, "Why would you do such a thing and risk losing your position? After all, you could have just confessed it to God and left it there." The answer is that I wanted to be right with God more than I wanted a position. At this point, I was willing to lose anything and everything to walk in the light as He is in the light. As I stood there before my pastor, a man whom I greatly respected and still do, he suddenly did something completely unexpected. He got up from his desk, walked around to where I was, and began to hug me. He then said these words: "I forgive you, Brother Robert, and so does God!" Wow! I was instantly set free from all guilt, shame, and uncleanness. I actually experienced what Jesus spoke of in John 20:22-23. As He prophetically released to them the Holy Spirit that was to come upon them days later, He commissioned them as well.

> *And when He had said this, He breathed on them, and said to them, "Receive the Holy Spirit. If you forgive the sins of any, they are forgiven them; if you retain the sins of any, they are retained."*

Jesus' commission to the disciples was to go forth and release people from their sins. Yes, there would be some who would be shut up in their sins. However, the majority would be released from their sin and have their destiny and future restored. This is what my pastor, James Walker, did for me on that day. He spoke the forgiveness of the Lord into my life and gave me a future! This all happened because I walked in the light as He is in the light. The result was His blood cleansed me from all sin. When we walk in a yielded manner before the Lord, we get the benefits of His speaking blood. This verse in 1 John 1:7 actually says in the Greek that the *blood of Jesus cleanses and keeps on cleansing from all sin.* This is why it is the blood that *speaks* and not just *has spoken.* If it said it is the blood that *spoke*, in a past tense way, it would only be sufficient for past sins. However, because it is the blood that *speaks,* it is for the past, the present, and even future sins.

However, if we are to get the effects of this blood, we must walk in the light as He is in the light. This means repentance. When we bring things to the light, it means we are acknowledging them and manifesting them. This is the position where the blood of sprinkling has the power to testify for us. We are told in John 3:16-19 that there is salvation for any and all who believe on the Son. However, if we choose darkness over light there is condemnation.

> *For God so loved the world that He gave His only begotten Son, that whoever believes in Him should not perish but have everlasting life. For God did not send His Son into the world to condemn the world, but that the world through Him might be saved.*
>
> *He who believes in Him is not condemned; but he who does not believe is condemned already, because he has not believed in the name of the only begotten Son of God. And this is the condemnation, that the light has come into the world, and men loved darkness rather than light, because their deeds were evil.*

When we believe in who Jesus is and what He has done, we gain eternal life. However, if we choose darkness and love it instead, we experience condemnation. When we walk in the light, the blood of Jesus speaks for us and brings us to place of forgiveness and cleansing. If we don't walk in the light and choose darkness instead, then we live a life under condemnation.

What is walking in the light? Is it perfect living? Absolutely not. Walking in the light is not *perfect living,* it is *honest living!* We are honest about our shortcomings and faults. We confess our sins. We allow the Holy Spirit to bring us to deep conviction and repentance. When we do this, we are walking in the light. This also empowers us to deal with our bloodline issues and get legal things in place that break the devil's assault against us and our future. Remember that when I began to repent for the covenants with demons in my bloodline, I felt deep sorrow and emotional distress. This was because the Holy Spirit had free access to my heart. The breakthroughs I experienced were immediate. I later would ask someone who was more advanced in the idea of the Courts of Heaven and bloodline cleansing why my breakthrough happened so fast. The reason for this question was because I had witnessed others not getting this level of victory. The one I asked said the reason for my immediate breakthrough was because I had "done the work." When I was told this, I didn't understand completely. However, as I considered it, I realized I had a history with God and a lifestyle of deep repentance before Him. My heart was easily moved before God. This has great value before the Lord.

In the days of Josiah, in 2 Kings 22:18-20, it shows us the power of a tender heart before God. Josiah had discovered the book of the Law in the Temple that was being restored. As the word of the Law was read before him, he began to realize how much they had broken God's word. When this happened, he came to deep repentance. God then said this about him:

> *But as for the king of Judah, who sent you to inquire of the Lord, in this manner you shall speak to him, "Thus says the Lord God of Israel: 'Concerning the words which you have heard—because your heart was tender, and you humbled yourself before the Lord when you heard what I spoke against this place and against its inhabitants, that they would become a desolation and a curse, and you tore your clothes and wept before Me, I also have heard you,' says the Lord. 'Surely, therefore, I will gather you to your fathers, and you shall be gathered to your grave in peace; and your eyes shall not see all the calamity which I will bring on this place.'" So they brought back word to the king.*

The Lord promised Josiah that God would spare him from the judgment to come. This was all because his heart was tender and he humbled himself before the Lord. This brokenness before God caused the Lord to respond to him in His mercy. When we have a heart that is yielded to the Lord, this allows God to move us to repentance quickly. As a result, we can repent for ourselves and our bloodline on a deeper dimension. Therefore, God is able to render verdicts for us because of this deep, sincere repentance. It agrees with the speaking blood and revokes legal claims the devil is making against us. Once this is done, we are freed from his accusations and able to move into the future designed by God for us. Verdicts from the Courts of Heaven will come quickly. This is what Jesus actually promised in Luke 18:6-8. We are told that there will be speedy results when we approach the Courts of Heaven.

> *Then the Lord said, "Hear what the unjust judge said. And shall God not avenge His own elect who cry out day and night to Him, though He bears long with them? I tell you that He will avenge them speedily. Nevertheless, when the Son of Man comes, will He really find faith on the earth?"*

Notice that those who cry out day and night get avenged speedily as they approach God as Judge. Crying out day and night speaks of having a history with the Lord in prayer. This is why I received such a quick result in the Courts of Heaven—it was because I had *done the work.* I had this history with God that had given me a place in this realm. My heart was tender and surrendered to the Lord. This is something we must develop and also always seek to maintain. When it is there, we can expect God and the heavenly realm to render verdicts for us.

We must guard ourselves against any hardness of heart. Usually hardness of heart is connected to unbelief. Mark 16:14-15 shows

Jesus challenging His disciples for their unbelief and hardness of heart.

> *Later He appeared to the eleven as they sat at the table; and He rebuked their unbelief and hardness of heart, because they did not believe those who had seen Him after He had risen. And He said to them, "Go into all the world and preach the gospel to every creature."*

The word *rebuke* is the Greek word *oneidizo.* It means "to chide, defame and to taunt." This doesn't seem like something Jesus would do, yet this is what the word means. I think the scripture is expressing to us the passion with which Jesus detests unbelief and hardness of heart. The word *hardness* is *skierokardia* in the Greek. It means "to be half-hearted and destitute of spiritual perception." Notice that Jesus was upset with them because they didn't believe those who had reported to have seen Him after the resurrection.

We do need to be discerning when people tell their supposed encounters with God. There are a lot of weird things that are propagated today as encounters with the Lord. There is also a lot of outright deception. We must be able to discern between the false and the true. However, we never want to develop a hard, skeptical heart that will not believe God. Jesus was clearly upset with His disciples because they didn't believe those who had seen Him. Jesus had a massive commission for the disciples to fulfill. This was going to require great faith and yielded hearts. This whole spirit of unbelief and hardness of heart had to be removed.

This was not the first time Jesus had challenged this in His disciples. In fact, this seems to have been an ongoing issue that Jesus was seeking to remove from the disciples. In Mark 8:14-21, we see the disciples in a boat and Jesus begins to talk with them about the influence of the Pharisees and Herod. They think He's talking about eating, when He's actually warning about letting these doctrines influence them.

> *Now the disciples had forgotten to take bread, and they did not have more than one loaf with them in the boat. Then He charged them, saying, "Take heed, beware of the leaven of the Pharisees and the leaven of Herod."*
>
> *And they reasoned among themselves, saying, "It is because we have no bread."*
>
> *But Jesus, being aware of it, said to them, "Why do you reason because you have no bread? Do you not yet perceive nor understand? Is your heart still hardened? Having eyes, do you not see? And having ears, do you not hear? And do you not remember? When I broke the five loaves for the five thousand, how many baskets full of fragments did you take up?"*
>
> *They said to Him, "Twelve."*
>
> *"Also, when I broke the seven for the four thousand, how many large baskets full of fragments did you take up?"*
>
> *And they said, "Seven."*
>
> *So He said to them, "How is it you do not understand?"*

Jesus seems to be exasperated with these men. Their spiritual discernment is nonexistent, it would appear. They think He's talking about eating bread when He is unlocking warnings concerning what they should be wary about. This is all because of a hardened heart. There is so much more we could look at in this idea. Suffice it to say, we must shake free from unbelief and a hardened heart. A tender heart before the Lord will allow us quick and speedy results in the Courts of Heaven. A skeptical, pessimistic heart is not a sign of maturity. It is actually just the opposite. We need a child's heart that is quick to respond to the Lord.

Let me cite two places where we see this kind of heart in operation. The first is when the disciples come back and are excited about the supernatural moving at their hands. Luke 10:17-21 shows Jesus getting excited about the disciples finally shaking free from the hardness that controlled their thinking.

> *Then the seventy returned with joy, saying, "Lord, even the demons are subject to us in Your name."*
>
> *And He said to them, "I saw Satan fall like lightning from heaven. Behold, I give you the authority to trample on serpents and scorpions, and over all the power of the enemy, and nothing shall by any means hurt you. Nevertheless do not rejoice in this, that the spirits are subject to you, but rather rejoice because your names are written in heaven."*
>
> *In that hour Jesus rejoiced in the Spirit and said, "I thank You, Father, Lord of heaven and earth, that You have hidden these things from the wise and prudent and revealed them to babes. Even so, Father, for so it seemed good in Your sight."*

Jesus had sent these seventy out to minister in His name. They came back with great excitement and joy because of the power of God moving at their hands. Jesus softly brought an adjustment to them concerning what this power they had seen was revealing. The fact that the demons were subject to them testified that their names were written in heaven. They had a place in the spirit that caused the demons to submit and obey. Jesus is admonishing them to recognize the deeper truth and be excited about this. Even though Jesus is instructing these disciples about what is really being revealed by the authority they've functioned in, He is excited that they are getting it. The Bible says Jesus *rejoiced.* The is the Greek word *agalliao.* It means to "jump for joy." Jesus was so excited that these hardened disciples were starting to soften. They were no longer pessimistic and skeptical. They weren't acting as the wise and prudent, judging everything incorrectly. They were developing a child's heart that would believe God. This greatly stirred Jesus' heart with joy. Their hearts were softening and heaven was responding.

The other place I would mention where we see Jesus excited about people losing a hardness of heart is in John 1:43-51. Philip recruits Nathanael to come and see who Jesus is. This scripture always stands out to me, because it reflects a heart so quick to believe God.

> *The following day Jesus wanted to go to Galilee, and He found Philip and said to him, "Follow Me." Now Philip was from Bethsaida, the city of Andrew and Peter. Philip found Nathanael and said to him, "We have found Him of whom Moses in the law, and also the prophets, wrote—Jesus of Nazareth, the son of Joseph."*
>
> *And Nathanael said to him, "Can anything good come out of Nazareth?"*
>
> *Philip said to him, "Come and see."*
>
> *Jesus saw Nathanael coming toward Him, and said of him, "Behold, an Israelite indeed, in whom is no deceit!"*
>
> *Nathanael said to Him, "How do You know me?"*
>
> *Jesus answered and said to him, "Before Philip called you, when you were under the fig tree, I saw you."*

> *Nathanael answered and said to Him, "Rabbi, You are the Son of God! You are the King of Israel!"*
>
> *Jesus answered and said to him, "Because I said to you, 'I saw you under the fig tree,' do you believe? You will see greater things than these." And He said to him, "Most assuredly, I say to you, hereafter you shall see heaven open, and the angels of God ascending and descending upon the Son of Man."*

Nathanael has his first encounter with Jesus. Through a word of knowledge, Jesus reveals to Nathanael where he was before Philip called him. This simple supernatural demonstration so touches Nathanael that he proclaims Jesus to be the Son of God. Jesus is impressed with Nathanael's quick discernment. Jesus therefore proclaims that because Nathanael has such a child's heart to believe quickly, he will see greater and greater things in the spirit world. He will actually see heaven opened and spiritual realms manifest to him. Wow! It is amazing how Jesus so much wants us to guard our heart against hardness and unbelief. He desires us to be discerning but not pessimistic. May we have the heart of a child that is soft, yielded, and pursuing the Lord. May we go after Him with a passion that allows a history with God. This will unlock the Courts of Heaven to us, for speedy and quick verdicts to be manifested.

> As I stand before the Courts of Heaven, I ask for deep repentance to be granted to me from the Lord. Forgive me, Lord, for any and all hardness of heart. I surrender to You and ask for these places of surrender to be my place. May I walk in the light as You are in the light. I repent for walking in darkness in any way. I bring all things into

the light and confess and agree with You concerning my sin and the sin of my bloodline. May Your blood speak for me in the Courts and grant God the legal right to forgive and cleanse me from all sin. May I have a history with You of repentance that is recorded in Your Courts. Therefore, as I stand before You, let this speak from the records of heaven on my behalf. Thank You, Lord, that my repentance allows the speaking blood of Your sacrifice to speak for me. May I be delivered from all condemnation of darkness and walk before You in true holiness. Let every accusation against me and my bloodline now be revoked and annulled in Jesus' Name. Let my future not be determined by the accusation, but by what is written in the Books of Heaven about me. Thank You, Lord, for the rendering of the verdicts and judgments that allow this to happen, in Jesus' Name, amen.

CHAPTER 8

RENOUNCING COVENANTS

Once we have repented of things in our life and our bloodline, we should then *renounce* any dependence on covenants with demons. In the next chapter, we will deal with giving back anything they say we have gained through these covenants. However, this is something we do after we have renounced any and every dependence on these devilish powers. We see this idea of renouncing things from our lives in 2 Corinthians 4:1-2.

> *Therefore, since we have this ministry, as we have received mercy, we do not lose heart. But we have renounced the hidden things of shame, not walking in craftiness nor handling the word of God deceitfully, but by manifestation of the truth commending ourselves to every man's conscience in the sight of God.*

Notice that Paul is saying there has been a renouncing of things of shame, craftiness, and deceit. This very much can be speaking of agreements with demons. Our words carry great power in the spirit world. When we use them to renounce agreements and covenants with demons, we are separating ourselves from their influence and effect.

The word *renounce* in this scripture is *apeipomen.* It means "to say off oneself, to disown." When we take our words and renounce something in the spirit realm, we are declaring it has no more power over us. The ability to separate from us existing rights of the adversary is found in renouncing. If we stop at repentance, this will not get the desired results. We must exercise our spiritual authority and renounce what the devil has used to hold us. If we are to do this effectively, we must know our spiritual authority and how words carry it. The renouncing or saying off of something in our life can be a recorded thing in the Courts of Heaven. Let's delve into the idea of renouncing something and seeing its power broken.

We see in Daniel 10:12 the power of words to summon spiritual powers. Angels came because of Daniel's words.

> *Then he said to me, "Do not fear, Daniel, for from the first day that you set your heart to understand, and to humble yourself before your God, your words were heard; and I have come because of your words."*

Daniel has been fasting and praying for 21 days at this point. Notice what this angel that has shown up says to Daniel. First of all, his words were heard from the first day. The fact that it took 21 days for the answer to arrive, because of warfare in the heavenlies, could have made Daniel think no one was listening. Yet when the angel shows up, it is verified that the moment Daniel started praying the words were heard. We must understand the operation of the spirit world by faith. We cannot give up quickly. We should keep pressing and pushing. Our words are being heard.

The next phrase the angel speaks is even more powerful, I think. He declares *I have come because of your words.* We must never underestimate the power of our words in the spirit world. This high-ranking angel has been sent because of the words of Daniel in prayer. What a powerful thought. Daniel's words moved the spirit world. David actually speaks of this as well in Psalm 18:6-19. He chronicles what happened in the spirit realm when his voice was heard in heaven.

In my distress I called upon the Lord,
And cried out to my God;
He heard my voice from His temple,
And my cry came before Him, even to His ears.

Then the earth shook and trembled;
The foundations of the hills also quaked and were shaken,
Because He was angry.
Smoke went up from His nostrils,
And devouring fire from His mouth;
Coals were kindled by it.
He bowed the heavens also, and came down
With darkness under His feet.
And He rode upon a cherub, and flew;
He flew upon the wings of the wind.
He made darkness His secret place;
His canopy around Him was dark waters
And thick clouds of the skies.
From the brightness before Him,
His thick clouds passed with hailstones and coals of fire.

The Lord thundered from heaven,
And the Most High uttered His voice,
Hailstones and coals of fire.
He sent out His arrows and scattered the foe,
Lightnings in abundance, and He vanquished them.

Then the channels of the sea were seen,
The foundations of the world were uncovered
At Your rebuke, O Lord,
At the blast of the breath of Your nostrils.

He sent from above, He took me;
He drew me out of many waters.
He delivered me from my strong enemy,
From those who hated me,
For they were too strong for me.
They confronted me in the day of my calamity,
But the Lord was my support.
He also brought me out into a broad place;
He delivered me because He delighted in me.

Notice the response of God to the voice of David. David's voice caused things to move in the unseen world. Wow. This is the power of our voice. If we could stop doubting this and move in faith, we would get an appreciation for the power of our words. They can carry the authority of God to move things around in the heavenly dimension. I took the time to quote this scripture because it does reveal the power of David's voice in the spirit world. It is quite amazing what can occur at our words.

Our words carry tremendous authority in the realm of the spirit. When we learn to use them correctly, we can see things unlocked. Of course this is what Jesus spoke of in Matthew 16:19. He was reiterating the power of our words to affect the unseen realm, which in return affects the natural realm.

And I will give you the keys of the kingdom of heaven, and whatever you bind on earth will be bound in heaven, and whatever you loose on earth will be loosed in heaven.

We have the authority granted by God to use these keys of authority to affect the unseen world. These words bind and loose and have legal connotations to them. The word *bind* is the Greek word *deo*. It means "to bind and put under obligation of the law." The word of God is the law. We have the right and authority from Jesus to put the devil under the obligation of God's law. This is what we are doing when we bind something. We are forcing it to obey the dictates of God's word. We cannot bind something just from our own desires. It has to be in agreement with the Word of the Lord. We are told in Matthew 12:28-29 that we can bind the strongman. Once this is done, we can take from the strongman all that he has taken himself.

> *But if I cast out demons by the Spirit of God, surely the kingdom of God has come upon you. Or how can one enter a strong man's house and plunder his goods, unless he first binds the strong man? And then he will plunder his house.*

We know Jesus is talking about casting out demons and removing devilish influence. He is very clear that the strong man must be first bound or put under the obligation of the law. If we are to accomplish this, we must first remove the legal claims that are allowing this strong man to steal from us. Once the legal claims are answered, we can then put this strong man under obligation to the law. We can demand that he cease and desist from operation. The problem most have in seeking to do this is the legal claims the devil is making that allow him to operate have not been revoked. Therefore, our words to bind him are ineffective. We must take the time and operate in enough discernment to remove the legal claims being made. This does involve our lives and our bloodline.

The other word Jesus used was the word *loose*. The Greek word for this is *luo*. It means "to loosen, undo, dissolve anything bound, tied, or compacted together; an assembly, i.e. to dismiss, break up; laws, as having a binding force, are likened to bonds." Notice that to loose has a legal meaning. From a legal perspective, this word means to dismiss a legal claim that has a binding force. In other words, satan makes cases against us that bind us. However, we have the right and authority to revoke and dismiss those legal claims. This can be accomplished after the grounds on which satan is making these claims are removed. For instance, if there is a covenant with demons that is being used to hold us in bondage, we must go through the process of removing this. We are then loosed from that which is providing the right of the devil to ruin our future.

Once these legal rights are revoked, we can make decrees and pronouncements that loose us or undo satan's legal claim. He will be required to let us, our future, and our lineage go. However, if he still has legal claims he is making, our decrees will have no power. Satan will simply keep doing what he is doing and will possibly backlash against us. We must realize that satan can only backlash against us if we have challenged something that still has a legal right, or we have stepped outside our realm of jurisdiction. This will result in an all-out attack from the devil. He will claim a legal right to consume us and devour us based on our illegal activity. This is why we are again told in 1 Peter 5:8 to be very careful not to give satan legal rights.

> *Be sober, be vigilant; because your adversary the devil walks about like a roaring lion, seeking whom he may devour.*

Remember that the word *adversary* is the Greek word *antidikos.* It means "one who brings a lawsuit or our legal opponent." This is who Peter said the devil is. Notice that this enemy operates from a legal place to be able to devour us. If satan has found any legal place, he will claim a right to devour us and what belongs to us. Notice he is seeking to devour. He cannot devour at will. He must find legal precedence to do it from. This involves covenants with demons and also iniquity in the bloodline. It also can involve his claiming rights to backlash against us. If we should challenge the devil prematurely, without taking away his legal claims, he will backlash. This is why I have people at times tell me they did everything I said and the attacks worsened. I immediately know this is a result of something still not dealt with in their life or bloodline. The devil cannot just attack. He must have a legal right he claims.

When we are seeking to operate in binding and loosing, we must make sure we have adequately dealt with the legal claims of the devil. Revelation 19:11 gives us the proper order for going to the battlefield in the spirit world and winning.

> *Now I saw heaven opened, and behold, a white horse. And He who sat on him was called Faithful and True, and in righteousness He judges and makes war.*

This is the way Jesus operates in the spirit world. Notice that He *judges* then *makes war. Judging* speaks of legal activity. *Making war* speaks of the battlefield. When we are aggressively declaring and decreeing, we are making war. We must first make sure that the right judgments are in place for this to be allowed. Otherwise we can suffer the backlash I'm speaking about. However, if we have taken the work of Jesus on the cross and used it to set legal things into place, we are now ready to make war. We can request of God to make judgments from His Courts and also make decrees in agreement with those judgments. This is critical for us to understand with regard to making decrees and renouncing things. In other words, we cannot judge what God is not judging. If we try to do this, we will be ineffective and open ourselves to backlash. We must be certain that God has rendered a judgment that allows us to operate as judges. We are told in 1 Corinthians 2:15-16 what is involved in us operating as judges in and from the Courts of Heaven.

> *But he who is spiritual judges all things, yet he himself is rightly judged by no one. For "who has known the mind of the Lord that he may instruct Him?" But we have the mind of Christ.*

The word *judge* in these verses is the Greek word *anakrino*. This word means "to sift; to examine closely; to scrutinize, scan; to try judicially; to judge, give judgment upon; to put questions, be inquisitive." This is the position we have been set in when we are spiritual. We are to be judges who can render judgments into place. From a place of discernment, we render judgments in agreement with the judgments of God. This is what allows what is done in heaven to have earthly effect. Notice also that we must have the mind of Christ to operate in this capacity. I'm not free to render judgments of my own volition or desire. My judgments must be in agreement with the judgments that God Himself is rendering. As someone once said, "I am here to do what God would do, if He were here to do it."

As I operate in the mind of Christ, any judgments I render will be in agreement with the Lord and His will. This will allow me to bind and loose effectively. I will be able to renounce any legal claim the devil is making. I will reorder the spiritual realm through the authority of my words. I speak off of myself any covenantal right satan is claiming over me and my bloodline. I am able to do this effectively because of the legal things that have been set into place. I am reclaiming my bloodline for and to the purposes of God. Every legal right satan has claimed is dismissed because of Jesus' blood that is speaking for me. All of this allows me to renounce covenants with demons and their effect against me and my bloodline. We undo what has been allowed to operate against us for generations. When we get these things spiritually into place, every force sent to devour us loses its right to function. We are freed and liberated to the purposes of God. God in His jealousy will arise and begin to reclaim our lives for His will.

> As we come to stand before Your Courts, Lord, I thank You that You have received my repentance. I even ask that all my repentance would speak in Your Courts to grant me status before You. As I stand in this place, I renounce all covenants with demon powers. I want nothing to do with them on any level. Remember, Lord, that I am Your servant and in covenant with You through the blood of Jesus. Therefore, Lord, arise and claim me for Your own. Let every covenant with demonic entities now be renounced and removed. From this place in the spirit I bind or set under the obligation of Your word every satanic power. They must line up and be regulated by the Word of God. I also loose or revoke any rights that powers of darkness are claiming. They lose their rights to function against me and my lineage. We belong to You. Arise, God, and execute Your judgments against all that would

seek to hinder Your will in my life. As a judge in the spirit world, I set in place Your judgments over my life and lineage. Let God arise and all His enemies be scattered, in Jesus' Name, amen!

CHAPTER 9

GIVE IT BACK!

As we undo these legal activities against us, we must also be willing to *give back* anything the devil claims we have gained through these covenants. The reason anyone would have entered a covenant with devils was to gain something from them. If we are to be fully freed, we must be willing to give up and give back whatever they would claim we might have gained. This can actually be a scary thing to do and pray. We can feel an uncertainty and fear of losing something. However, this is where a trust and a confidence in the goodness of God is essential. When I know how good God is, I will have no problem in letting go of what demons might claim to have provided. I know that ultimately every good and perfect gift comes from God. James 1:16-17 makes the emphatic statement concerning this.

> *Do not be deceived, my beloved brethren. Every good gift and every perfect gift is from above, and comes down from the Father of lights, with whom there is no variation or shadow of turning.*

If it is good, it came from God. The devil might claim credit for it, but the origin is from the Lord. We should give thanks to Him and realize demons have no power or will to do good from a pure heart. Anything they claim we have gained is for the purpose of control or to possess us and our lineage. This is the whole reason for a trade being made with the demonic. Ultimately the purpose of a trade with the demonic causes us to lose and not to gain.

We can see in the scripture where God's people credited someone other than God with doing them good. In Hosea 2:2-13 we have insight on *why* we must give back anything the devil has claimed we gained from him. If we don't, the devil has a legal right to exact against us the word of the Lord. He can claim before the Courts of Heaven that this is what was declared would happen.

> *"Bring charges against your mother, bring charges;*
> *For she is not My wife, nor am I her Husband!*
> *Let her put away her harlotries from her sight,*
> *And her adulteries from between her breasts;*
> *Lest I strip her naked*
> *And expose her, as in the day she was born,*
> *And make her like a wilderness,*
> *And set her like a dry land,*
> *And slay her with thirst.*
>
> *"I will not have mercy on her children,*
> *For they are the children of harlotry.*
> *For their mother has played the harlot;*
> *She who conceived them has behaved shamefully.*
> *For she said, 'I will go after my lovers,*
> *Who give me my bread and my water,*
> *My wool and my linen,*
> *My oil and my drink.'*
>
> *"Therefore, behold,*
> *I will hedge up your way with thorns,*

And wall her in,
So that she cannot find her paths.
She will chase her lovers,
But not overtake them;
Yes, she will seek them, but not find them.
Then she will say,
'I will go and return to my first husband,
For then it was better for me than now.'
For she did not know
That I gave her grain, new wine, and oil,
And multiplied her silver and gold—
Which they prepared for Baal.

"Therefore I will return and take away
My grain in its time
And My new wine in its season,
And will take back My wool and My linen,
Given to cover her nakedness.
Now I will uncover her lewdness in the sight of her lovers,
And no one shall deliver her from My hand.
I will also cause all her mirth to cease,
Her feast days,
Her New Moons,
Her Sabbaths—
All her appointed feasts.

"And I will destroy her vines and her fig trees,
Of which she has said,
'These are my wages that my lovers have given me.'
So I will make them a forest,
And the beasts of the field shall eat them.
I will punish her

For the days of the Baals to which she burned incense.
She decked herself with her earrings and jewelry,
And went after her lovers;
But Me she forgot," says the Lord.

There are several things to notice in these scriptures. Before we go into this, however, let me establish that the devil, as our accuser, uses the word of God against us. He makes cases based on what is recorded in God's law and word. Remember that satan is called the accuser in Revelation 12:10-11. He is the one who brings accusations against us day and night.

> *Then I heard a loud voice saying in heaven, "Now salvation, and strength, and the kingdom of our God, and the power of His Christ have come, for the accuser of our brethren, who accused them before our God day and night, has been cast down. And they overcame him by the blood of the Lamb and by the word of their testimony, and they did not love their lives to the death."*

The word *accuser* is the Greek word *katagoros.* It means "a complainant at law." In other words, it speaks of someone who is bringing a legal charge in a court against someone. When the Bible says that satan is the *accuser of the brethren,* it is unveiling that he is operating from a legal position to assault us. Per this scripture, he is constantly and consistently bringing cases and evidence against us. Through these cases, he is seeking to deny us the promises of God that are ours as New Covenant believers. However, he is also putting limits on us that constrain and restrict us from all that is meant to be ours from God.

The Greek word *katagoros* is the word we get our word *categorize* from. This means that through his accusations we are denied the territory, influence, and impact we are to have. This is a result of his accusations against us. This will usually bring us to a place of frustration, anger, and ultimately resignation that this is our lot in life. We know because of the revelation of God the place ordained by God for us. However, we cannot seem to get into that place. The devil will seek to wear us out and bring us to this position of giving up and quitting. The accuser/*katagoros* has to be silenced for us to obtain what is meant for us by God. He does not let go of his legal claim against us until we require him to.

One of the main things the devil uses to build cases against us is the word of the Lord. We see this in John 8:3-5 where the religious leaders of Israel are desiring to bring punishment against the woman caught in adultery.

> *Then the scribes and Pharisees brought to Him a woman caught in adultery. And when they had set her in the midst, they said to Him, "Teacher, this woman was caught in adultery, in the very act. Now Moses, in the law, commanded us that such should be stoned. But what do You say?"*

What the leaders were really after was a reason to accuse Jesus and bring charges against Him. If He defended the woman, then He would be accused of nullifying the law given through Moses. If He agreed she should be stoned, then He was no different than the religious bigots bringing the charge. We know that Jesus was able to listen to His Father and give them an answer that brought conviction to their hearts. However, what I would like to point out is that the accusation the accusers were bringing was based on the word of God the woman had broken. This is exactly what the devil does with us. He tempts us and presses us to disobey God. Then when we do, he uses our disobedience to bring accusation and build cases against us. He also demands the right to bring the punishment the word of God declares connected to our rebellion. This is why we should obey God, and also be quick to repent if we ever fall into places of sin. The devil is desiring to use this as a right to demand the consequences of our sin be visited upon us.

With that said, let's look at the scripture from Hosea where there is a *charge* being brought against Israel. There are several things that are seen here that we should pay attention to and take before the Courts of Heaven. First of all, we see that there is a *charge* being brought against this people. Hosea 2:2 shows God is declaring that the nation of Israel is worthy of legal charges being brought.

> *Bring charges against your mother, bring charges;*
> *For she is not My wife, nor am I her Husband!*
> *Let her put away her harlotries from her sight,*
> *And her adulteries from between her breasts.*

God is accusing Israel, as the mother, of spiritual adultery and serving other gods and idols. He is bringing a charge against her that she is unfaithful to Him as her husband. At this stage, the Lord is even saying they are no longer married. I want us to notice, however, what one of the charges being leveled against Israel is. According Hosea 2:5, Israel is accrediting *her lovers* with what she has.

> *For their mother has played the harlot;*
> *She who conceived them has behaved shamefully.*
> *For she said, "I will go after my lovers,*

Who give me my bread and my water,
My wool and my linen,
My oil and my drink."

Israel declared that what she had came from the demons who empowered the idol worship of Israel. Israel said that it wasn't God who gave her these blessings, it was the idols she chose to serve. This is echoed again in Hosea 2:12.

And I will destroy her vines and her fig trees,
Of which she has said,
"These are my wages that my lovers have given me."
So I will make them a forest,
And the beasts of the field shall eat them.

Israel's unwillingness to acknowledge God in her blessings shows her not giving back what has been claimed by the demons. However, we know that in reality these blessings didn't come from demons they were in covenant with, but from God. The Lord even says this as well in Hosea 2:8. He points out that what Israel thinks came from demons and idols actually was the result of God's blessings.

For she did not know
That I gave her grain, new wine, and oil,
And multiplied her silver and gold—
Which they prepared for Baal.

The Lord was the source of the blessings, even though the demons claimed to have done it. Israel was not acknowledging where it had come from. When we are annulling covenants with demons from our bloodline, we must be willing to give back anything and everything that they say we gained from them. If we don't do this, it gives the devil a legal right to visit consequences upon us. Please remember that God, from a New Testament perspective, only does good. However, the devil takes opportunity from the word of God to bring trouble upon us. We must be willing to give back whatever "blessing" these demons claim, in order to fully annul any legal right they are claiming against us.

Again, here in Hosea 2, we see the results of not giving back what demons claim and accuse us with in the Courts of Heaven. The things that God says will be done to Israel, because she acknowledged demons as her source rather than God, can be visited upon us if we don't give it back!

There are at least seven things that the devil could have a legal right to visit upon us should we not give back what demons claim we gained through covenant with them. As we see covenants annulled with demons from our bloodline, we should give back whatever they say we gained. This will fully undo any covenant with the demon powers that is allowing them to claim rights over us and our lineage.

The first thing mentioned is that we can be *stripped naked.* Hosea 2:2-3 mentions this as punishment for covenants with demonic powers.

> *Bring charges against your mother, bring charges;*
> *For she is not My wife, nor am I her Husband!*
> *Let her put away her harlotries from her sight,*
> *And her adulteries from between her breasts;*
> *Lest I strip her naked*
> *And expose her, as in the day she was born,*
> *And make her like a wilderness,*

And set her like a dry land,
And slay her with thirst.

Stripped naked can mean the loss of everything. Several years ago, a fellow minister who operated from an apostolic perspective was stripped naked. It appeared this man was much more impactful and powerful than me in ministry and influence. He definitely had a realm of impact I didn't have at that time. We walked in a measure of relationship, as I sought to build the church in Waco, Texas, that I was commissioned by God to build. This man was about 100 miles away in a larger city. We had a more-than-casual relationship, but he definitely saw himself as my superior.

One night I had a dream that this man was stripped naked and was in Mary's and my bed. When I realized this in the dream I was offended and upset because my wife was present. However, in the dream I realized there was nothing sexual about the situation. I knew this man had been stripped naked and was left with nothing. The next day, I called him and told him the dream. He was polite enough but acknowledged no real sense of God showing him something. Literally within days, the *team* associated with this man rose up against him and kicked him out of the church he had started and pioneered. They were able to legally do this because of the constitution and bylaws they had in operation. It allowed the elders/leaders to vote out this leader if they chose. This man lost his house, church, ministry, reputation, and almost lost his family and marriage. He and his family struggled immensely. They went from great blessings, wealth, and influence to absolutely nothing.

They were still living in the city where this occurred, but wanted to move away for a fresh start. They were considering several options. I was wondering if I should offer them a place in Waco, Texas. I really didn't want to, but wondered if it was the intent of God or not. I was a little concerned about bringing this man to Waco and the possible negative effect it might have. Then the Lord reminded me of my dream. I felt I heard Him say about my dream, "*He was in your bed.*" I knew God was telling me that I was to extend an invitation for this man and his family to relocate to Waco, Texas. Someone being in *your bed* speaks of your place of authority, domain, and provision. I therefore extended the invitation and they immediately responded that they wanted to come. They did, in fact, move to Waco and it became a place of restoration and healing for them to re-launch in life and ministry. This all happened because of a dream that unveiled someone being stripped naked before it happened.

In Hosea, this is the result of a covenant with demons and an unwillingness to give back what had been gained. I didn't understand the Courts of Heaven when what I just described happened. However, my suspicion is that there was something in the bloodline that allowed the devil to strip this man and his family of what they had. It could have been, and most probably was, a covenant with demon powers that gave them the legal right to bring such destruction. This covenant would have been in the bloodline or ancestry of this man. However, there is no time limit on covenants in the spirit world. This is because covenants made in the spirit dimension are forever, or until they are revoked and annulled. God declared in Deuteronomy 7:9 that He is faithful to keep His covenant for a thousand generations.

> *Therefore know that the Lord your God, He is God, the faithful God who keeps covenant and mercy for a thousand generations with those who love Him and keep His commandments.*

This means that God will be faithful to His word toward those He gave it to. The psalmist picked up this word and reiterated it in Psalm 105:8-10. He shows that when God is said to keep His word for a thousand generations, it means forever!

> *He remembers His covenant forever,*
> *The word which He commanded, for a thousand generations,*
> *The covenant which He made with Abraham,*
> *And His oath to Isaac,*
> *And confirmed it to Jacob for a statute,*
> *To Israel as an everlasting covenant.*

So to be clear, when God remembers the word He gave for a thousand generations, it means it is an everlasting covenant. This is the standard and nature of God. When someone makes a covenant with devilish powers, the devil claims this right as well. God's word establishes this as the standard. Therefore, the devil claims this as the right he also has. This means covenants with the devil never vanish over time. They are perpetual and active until someone nullifies them. Just to be clear, this is not the standard for iniquity. They do have time limits on them when we know how to set God's word and standard in place. However, covenants with demons have to be annulled and have their rights revoked. We will deal with iniquity in later chapters. If we know how to undo these covenants and give back in the spirit world anything gained, we can avert the tragedies and devouring power of the adversary against us.

A second consequence of not giving back what satan says we have gained is we can been *slain with thirst.* Hosea 2:3 shows God releasing this as a judgment against what is in covenant with demons. If there is a covenant with demons in our bloodline because it hasn't been thoroughly dealt with by giving back what satan claims we gained, we can suffer this.

> *Lest I strip her naked*
> *And expose her, as in the day she was born,*
> *And make her like a wilderness,*
> *And set her like a dry land,*
> *And slay her with thirst.*

The Lord declared that things would dry up and it would result in us dying from thirst. Dying from thirst can speak of a lack of deep satisfaction and fulfillment. We know this is true because when the opposite is spoken of—being refreshed and fulfilled—it is speaking of refreshing and living waters. In Jeremiah 2:13 we see the Lord declaring Himself as the fountain of living waters whom His people have forsaken.

> *For My people have committed two evils:*
> *They have forsaken Me, the fountain of living waters,*
> *And hewn themselves cisterns—broken cisterns that can hold no water.*

As the fountain of living waters, the Lord refreshes our soul and brings life to us. When we are *slain with thirst in a dry land,* it means things are drying up and there is no satisfaction in us. This leads to many places of trouble for us. When there is no deep place of satisfaction and fulfillment, we have no real meaning and purpose in life. This can lead to giving ourselves over to fleshly lust and enticements. This is why Proverbs 29:18 lets us know that without vision and purpose, restraints are cast off. This can be the result of things drying up in our souls. God declares it can become so bad that we are actually slain from thirst.

> *Where there is no revelation, the people cast off restraint;*
> *But happy is he who keeps the law.*

The devil can have a right to produce this in us when we haven't given back what he declares we have gained. Our spiritual condition becomes one of dryness, parched places, and desert experiences. May we annul all covenants with demon powers and give back whatever they say we might have gained.

A third result of a covenant not completely revoked with demon powers is no mercy for our children. Hosea 2:4-5 makes a terrible statement against the children of those who have covenants with demons.

> *I will not have mercy on her children,*
> *For they are the children of harlotry.*
> *For their mother has played the harlot;*
> *She who conceived them has behaved shamefully.*
> *For she said, "I will go after my lovers,*
> *Who give me my bread and my water,*
> *My wool and my linen,*
> *My oil and my drink."*

This statement in the word of God gives the devil legal right to visit this against our children if there are covenants with demons intact. Notice that clearly the covenant with demons is a result of seeing the satanic as the source. This has to be undone or our lineage will be claimed by the devil. This was something that I experienced firsthand. The covenant with demons in my bloodline gave the devil the legal right to claim me and my children. Only when it was annulled did my children and I come free. Mary and I had raised our children with a godly standard. We had raised them according to Ephesians 6:4. They had been brought up in church, Christian school, and any and every other influence that was possible to press them toward the Lord. Yet as they reached adulthood, they had started making unwise and unchristian decisions. We have six children, and all of them were not serving God the way they should have been. There were divorces occurring, pregnancy outside of marriage, drug addictions, and other things afflicting our heritage. Mary and I thought we must have been the worst parents who ever lived.

As I shared previously, our kids were going in the wrong directions, and we didn't seem to be able to stop it. I had no idea that this was the result not of our parenting skills, but of a covenant with demons that was giving them legal rights to claim our children. This was a consequence of whoever had made a covenant with Parax in our bloodline in previous generations. I discovered that when there is a covenant with demons in the bloodline, it grants satanic powers the right to claim and take captive our lineage. We do not get the enjoyment that our children are meant to bring us. Deuteronomy 28:32 tells us that a part of the curse is our children will be taken away and we will have no power to do anything about it.

> *Your sons and your daughters shall be given to another people, and your eyes shall look and fail with longing for them all day long; and there shall be no strength in your hand.*

Notice that our children will be taken by other people. In other words, they will fall under the influence of someone else. We will desire them and long for what we used to have with them, but have no power to restore it. They will seem to be beyond our reach. They will be hardened to our pleas for them to walk with God and serve

Him. This is where our children were. We couldn't understand how this could be happening. I didn't realize they were under a devilish influence that was claiming legal rights because of this covenant in my ancestry. These powers said that legally my children belonged to them because of covenants in our history. This was giving them the right to enact the curses spoken of in scripture. Of course, Deuteronomy 28 is the chapter where the curses are mentioned against those who disobey God. The people in my bloodline who had dedicated our bloodline to demonic powers had done this. Therefore, the powers of darkness were claiming a legal right to claim my children. Also, in Deuteronomy 28:41 we are told we will lose our children to captivity as a result of the legal right to land curses because of covenants with demons.

> *You shall beget sons and daughters, but they shall not be yours; for they shall go into captivity.*

When the Bible says *they will not be yours,* it is declaring something else will control them and possess them. They will be captive to immorality, addictions, and other forms of control. Again, this is what was occurring with our children. It was a grievous thing to Mary and me. We knew the choices our children were making was going to bring great sorrow and heartache to them. Yet there seemed to be nothing we could do to break the "captivity" they were in.

This is when I had my first encounter in the Courts of Heaven. If you will remember, this was where it was revealed that there was a covenant with the demon god Parax. When I annulled the covenant with Parax and asked for a legal rendering against it, I thought it was only to stop the attacks against me and the ministry. However, without telling my children anything I had done or discovered, they all began to come back to the Lord. In a very short period of time, they all were serving God and desiring His destiny for their lives. Today, out of the six children we have, three sons pastor their own churches full time. My two daughters work full time for my ministry. My oldest son has been very successful in the business world. We watched as our children all turned toward the Lord with great aggression. This was not the result of nagging, preaching, pressing, or manipulating them in any way. It came when the legal claims of the devil were revoked. The covenantal rights were revoked when we repented, renounced, and gave back anything they claimed we had gained. So it can be with you and your family as well.

> Lord, as we come before Your Courts, let it be known that I am in covenant with You through the blood of the covenant that Jesus provided on the cross. I am Your possession because of Jesus' blood and body for me. Let it also be known that I have repented of any agreement with demonic powers through my own activity and the activity in my ancestry and bloodline. I repent for any and all covenants made with demonic powers through my sins, transgressions, deceits, and trades made in the spirit realm, whether on purpose or by other activities. Let it be known that I repent for myself and my bloodline concerning these things. I also renounce and speak off of me every agreement with devilish entities that would try to claim rights over me and my lineage! From this place in the spirit realm I now ***give back*** anything the devils, demons, satanic realm, or powers of darkness

claim I have gained from them and this covenant. I want nothing from them. I only want what belongs to me through the graciousness of God and His covenant with me.

I therefore ask, as I stand before Your Courts, for a judgment rendered that would annul all covenant rights the devil would claim against me and my lineage. I ask that any right he claims to strip me naked is now revoked. He cannot destroy what You have entrusted me with. Ministry, business, family, reputation, influence, wealth, and accumulation will not be removed. He loses the right to take from me anything I have gained through You. Let it be known that You are the One who has blessed me with this and not the powers of darkness.

I also ask that any right the demonic claims to slay me with thirst is revoked and removed. You, Lord, are my fountain of living waters. You are the One who satisfies my soul. I will not seek to fill the emptiness with lustful things. I am Your servant and You refresh me with Your goodness and graciousness. Let any claim the powers of darkness make to slay me with thirst now be revoked. I have given back anything it claims I have gained from it. Allow the presence and power of the Holy Spirit to now move in me and through me as a refreshing water of life. Let the river of God flow in my soul from the innermost part of my being.

I also ask for a judgment from the Courts of Heaven to free my children, lineage, and inheritance from the powers of darkness. Let any legal claim they are making against me or my children, grandchildren, great-grandchildren, and beyond be now revoked, removed, and annulled. These are dedicated and given to the Lord as a part of my bloodline. The powers of darkness lose every legal claim to bring my children, grandchildren, great-grandchildren, and beyond into captivity. They are completely freed from the devil's claims and influence. They have full destinies in God and shall fulfill them. Let it be recorded in Your Courts that I give back anything the devil says I have gained from covenants with him. I do not want anything that he would have given me. I only want what belongs to me by my covenant with God the Father through the blood of Jesus. Therefore, let any and all covenant rights satan and his powers would claim be revoked, removed, and annulled this day against me and my lineage. In Jesus' Name, amen!

CHAPTER 10

RETURNING ANYTHING GAINED!

As I said previously, there are at least seven different things that can occur against us when we don't give back what the devil claims we have gotten from him. We have dealt with three in the previous chapter. We pinpointed being stripped naked, dying of thirst, and losing our children. We want to deal with the remaining four in this chapter. This can occur if we don't sufficiently deal with covenants with demons by giving back what they say we gained from them. This is chronicled in Hosea 2 as the people of God claimed their *blessings* had come from idols that were empowering demons. As a result, God had purposed to judge Israel for this activity. Even though we are in the New Testament era, the devil will take what God has said and claim a legal right to visit this on people. This is why we must repent and give back anything the demonic says we have gained. Otherwise, the devil will use this as a legal right to bring these destructions into our lives, families, and circumstances.

The fourth consequence of not completely dealing with covenants with demons by not giving back what they say we gained is that the way is blocked to our success and future. Hosea 2:6 clearly states that as a result of the claim that what we have was a result of demonic blessing, our the path to success and influence is hindered.

> *Therefore, behold,*
> *I will hedge up your way with thorns,*
> *And wall her in,*
> *So that she cannot find her paths.*

If we have not given back what the demonic says we gained, they have a legal right to hinder our success and prosperity. We are promised by God that we will have good success and a great future. Joshua 1:8 gives us the promise of a prosperous way and good success.

> *This Book of the Law shall not depart from your mouth, but you shall meditate in it day and night, that you may observe to do according to all that is written in it. For then you will make your way prosperous, and then you will have good success.*

We are told that if we meditate and renew our minds with the word of God and observe and obey all that is written, we will have prosperity and success. Yet I had definitely done this, but I constantly saw delay and frustration rather than success. When I discovered the Courts of Heaven and cleansing of the bloodline, this was when the word of God was fulfilled. I found out that you can have a true promise from God and not see it happen because of a legal case against you in the spirit realm. Even though you are fulfilling the word concerning that promise, it will not happen if there is a legal claim against you. Only when we fully annul any demonic covenant by giving back what they claim we gained will that covenant be revoked. This will allow you to come into the full blessings of prosperity and success. You will be able to find your path and make your way prosperous. This definitely happened in my life. When I repented, renounced, and gave back what supposedly was gained from the demonic, new levels of opportunity and prosperity began to come.

We had been under great assault and attack. In particular, there were tales and stories being told about us by some very high-profile people. They had heard things that were not true and were repeating this as fact. Of course, none of these had followed the mandates of scripture. Jesus was very clear about how to handle issues like this. Never did He say repeat it as fact to do the most damage you can to a person. No! He revealed in Matthew 18:15-17 how to handle these situations. This was so the redemptive purposes of God might be served, rather that the destruction of the devil.

> *Moreover if your brother sins against you, go and tell him his fault between you and him alone. If he hears you, you have gained your brother. But if he will not hear, take with you one or two more, that "by the mouth of two or three witnesses every word may be established." And if he refuses to hear them, tell it to the church. But if he refuses even to hear the church, let him be to you like a heathen and a tax collector.*

First of all, Jesus said if the *sin is against you.* If it's not against you, it's none of your business. We should keep it *out of our mouth!* Why do we persist in disobeying the word of God in these matters? If the problem isn't affecting you or me, we should leave it alone. However, if we are affected by this issue, we aren't to talk to others about it, but go to the person who we think is guilty of it. Jesus was clear. Go to the person *alone.* We must first deal with it in privacy before ever bringing it to a public forum. If it can't be brought to a conclusion in private then we follow the other dictates laid out by Jesus. When we violate these principles, we are giving the devil the right to legally devour us. Our disobedience to the word of God allows this. There will be a case against us that allows devouring to occur from the satanic realm.

As a result of these clear principles not being adhered to, there was great destruction released into our lives and ministry. People began to believe the lies that were told about us. We were never asked about any of it. The natural outgrowth of all this was doors being shut, opportunities removed, and a stifling of what God had called us to do. Then I discovered the Courts of Heaven. When I annulled the covenant with demons, including giving back what they claimed I had gained, great breakthroughs started to come. Even though the words of those who were speaking against us were not repented of, other doors began to open that gave me a worldwide effect! This is what the Lord promised in Revelation 3:8.

> *I know your works. See, I have set before you an open door, and no one can shut it; for you have a little strength, have kept My word, and have not denied My name.*

Notice that God promises to open doors *no one can shut.* The Lord began to open doors for us that those who told lies about us couldn't shut! This is because I gave back what the demonic said I gained. Therefore, my way was not hedged up, I was not walled in, and I could find my path. This was because I gave back what they said I gained, and the covenant with demons was completely annulled. Notice in Revelation that as a result of our works being approved by God, an open door that cannot be shut is set in place. We have to *see it.* When we do we can move through it and into the future God has for us. The devil has no legal right to prohibit it any further. We are no longer hedged in but free to move into prosperity, success, and the future God has for us.

The fifth thing that can happen when we don't fully deal with demonic covenants through giving back what they claim we gained is lack of prosperity. Hosea 2:8-9 shows that because they didn't know the real source of what they had, prosperity was removed.

> *For she did not know*
> *That I gave her grain, new wine, and oil,*
> *And multiplied her silver and gold—*
> *Which they prepared for Baal.*
>
> *Therefore I will return and take away*
> *My grain in its time*
> *And My new wine in its season,*
> *And will take back My wool and My linen,*
> *Given to cover her nakedness.*

Our lack of understanding of the real source of blessing into our lives can give the devil the legal right to steal away our prosperity. Even though we are promised prosperity as New Testament believers, we cannot experience it because of legal claims against us. Prosperity is one of the things the devil will seek to legally remove from us as a result of covenants with devils. There are several reason for this. When we don't prosper, we cannot help establish God's covenant purposes in the earth. The Lord needs a wealthy, prosperous people to accomplish His will through. Deuteronomy 8:18 clearly depicts this truth.

> *And you shall remember the Lord your God, for it is He who gives you power to get wealth, that He may establish His covenant which He swore to your fathers, as it is this day.*

We are given power to get wealth when we *remember* the Lord our God. The truth of God about prosperity is revealed in this scripture. Notice that wealth is necessary to establish God's covenant and fulfill the promises of God. It takes money to preach the gospel, minister to God's people, and reclaim society. God desires the masses to be touched, affected, and redeemed. Without finances, this is greatly hindered and even completely stopped from occurring. The devil knows this. Therefore, he looks for legal rights to stop the prosperity of God's people. If this can be accomplished, satan is greatly empowered to restrict the advancement of God's kingdom.

There was a reason why God gave a bunch of Jewish slaves the wealth of Egypt when they were delivered. They would spend 40 years in the wilderness. Why would they need the wealth of Egypt in desert places? It was so they would have what was needed to *finance* the building of God's tabernacle among them. As a result of what they carried out of Egypt, the dwelling place of God among them was built. Remember that they had been instructed to ask the Egyptians for their wealth. When they did this, to everyone's dismay, they actually were given it. When this happened, they spoiled Egypt and plundered the Egyptians. Later on in the wilderness, the tabernacle was built from these treasures. When it came time to build it, these Jewish people began to bring their treasures with such generosity that there was more than enough. In fact, according to Exodus 36:4-7 we are told of this great liberality of giving.

> *Then all the craftsmen who were doing all the work of the sanctuary came, each from the work he was doing, and they spoke to Moses, saying, "The people bring much more than enough for the service of the work which the Lord commanded us to do."*
>
> *So Moses gave a commandment, and they caused it to be proclaimed throughout the camp, saying, "Let neither man nor woman do any more work for the offering of the sanctuary." And the people were restrained from bringing, for the material they had was sufficient for all the work to be done—indeed too much.*

God's plan for financing the work of His church in the earth was to do it *through* His people. The Bible actually refers to His people in the wilderness as His church. Acts 7:38 makes this statement concerning the people who were in these desert places.

> *This is he who was in the congregation in the wilderness with the Angel who spoke to him on Mount Sinai, and with our fathers, the one who received the living oracles to give to us.*

The word *congregation* is the Greek word *ecclesia.* This is the word Jesus used to describe the church He would build. The church/*ecclesia* that Jesus builds is a governmental people commissioned to expand and bring increase to the kingdom of God in the earth. We are to see individuals reached and impacted, but also culture changed as well. Matthew 16:18-19 lets us know that the church Jesus builds is one that expands the rule of God into the cultures of the earth.

> *And I also say to you that you are Peter, and on this rock I will build My church, and the gates of Hades shall not prevail against it. And I will give you the keys of the kingdom of heaven, and whatever you bind on earth will be bound in heaven, and whatever you loose on earth will be loosed in heaven.*

In other words, it is through the church/*ecclesia* that what God desires in the earth will be seen. We as His church are here to see earth look more like heaven than like hell. This requires finances, wealth, and the prosperity of God's people. Therefore, the devil is looking for legal reasons to stop this prosperity from occurring. One of the ways he does this is through the covenants with demons in our bloodlines. When these are undone completely, we will prosper and increase in wealth. This requires the giving back of anything satan says we have gained. Any trade he says we made must be undone and totally annulled. This will remove his legal claims to hinder our prosperity.

Another diabolical reason satan loves to hinder our prosperity is to demoralize us as the people of God. Poverty, lack, and need are used by satan to discourage and disillusion us. This is what happened to the children of Israel in the bondage of Egypt. Their poverty and cruel service they endured took their passion for life and God out of them. We see in Exodus 6:6-9 the lack of responsiveness that was in them because of the rigors of service forced on them.

> *Therefore say to the children of Israel: "I am the Lord; I will bring you out from under the burdens of the Egyptians, I will rescue you from their bondage, and I will redeem you with an outstretched arm and with great*

> *judgments. I will take you as My people, and I will be your God. Then you shall know that I am the Lord your God who brings you out from under the burdens of the Egyptians. And I will bring you into the land which I swore to give to Abraham, Isaac, and Jacob; and I will give it to you as a heritage: I am the Lord." So Moses spoke thus to the children of Israel; but they did not heed Moses, because of anguish of spirit and cruel bondage.*

Moses is reciting to the people the promises of God. These people, who are beset by the poverty of slaves and the hard service, can't even respond. Sometimes even the promises of God have no power to move us until poverty, need, and the hardship it causes are removed. The devil loves to harass us with lack and need. He takes out of us the ability even to respond to the good word of God. We must see revoked and removed all legal claims of the enemy to bring us into emptiness. When these things are taken out of our life and our bloodline, we will be freed to prosper. Even the poverty of generations can be ended because the legal rights to hold us there are annulled.

It is God's will to prosper us for His purposes and our sakes. He desires us to increase on every level. Some common ideas spawned by the religious spirit need to be undone. The whole idea that it is spiritual to be poor is wrong and literally the lie of the devil. Paul tells us in 1 Timothy 6:17-19 some practical advice to those who have prospered.

> *Command those who are rich in this present age not to be haughty, nor to trust in uncertain riches but in the living God, who gives us richly all things to enjoy. Let them do good, that they be rich in good works, ready to*

> *give, willing to share, storing up for themselves a good foundation for the time to come, that they may lay hold on eternal life.*

As those whom God will prosper once the legal claims of the devil are revoked from us, we should adhere to this wisdom. We are not to place our confidence in our wealth. Our confidence and trust must always be in the Lord. Notice also that God has no problem with *things*. In fact, this scripture says He gives us *things* to enjoy. It is His delight to bless His children in this life. As long as our hearts belong to Him and not the things, He greatly enjoys watching us enjoy His blessings. Notice that how we handle our finances can cause us to have the established future that is designed for us. There is a responsibility that is given to us when we have prosperity. What we do with it determines the future we will have, even in eternity. We are to always be laying hold of eternal life. While we enjoy His blessings in this life, we are to be doing His kingdom work as well. This will provide for us a good future even into eternity!

I heard a very powerful story that illustrates this principle. There was a prophetic man we will call Hank. He had ministered often in a particular nation. In this nation, there is not a liberality in giving, even though there would be resources that would allow this. I have also ministered in this first-world country quite a bit and know this to be true. I would have to treat the ministry there as a mission trip and finance it myself when I went there. This was true for Hank as well. He had spoken and ministered in this nation quite a bit. There were never much offerings given, because this was the nature of this country. However, this man ministered in a certain location and to his amazement was greatly blessed and honored with a sizable offering. He was so excited because for the first time ever, he was shown generosity. He went from the meetings to the train station to go to his next destination.

As is the practice in this nation, he had the offering in cash with him. As he sat in the train waiting for it to board and leave, what appeared to be a homeless person came and stood at the open window of the train. This indigent person stood on the outside looking into the train and asked Hank for some money. The moment he did, the Lord said to Hank, "Give him the money, Hank." Hank was completely troubled. He actually said no to this voice, hoping it was the devil telling him to do this thing. However, as Hank sat there waiting in the train to leave, the indigent man kept standing at the window looking in. Hank heard the voice again, "Give him the money, Hank." Again, Hank resisted the voice and began to reason with the Lord over why this was wrong. The train began to move. One final time Hank heard the voice. "Give him the money, Hank!"

As the train slowly picked up speed, Hank jumped from his seat, shoved the money out the window, and said "Here! Take it!" The seemingly homeless man looked back in the window and said, "Thank you, Hank!" Suddenly, Hank recognized it was an angel in the form of an indigent person. Hank had passed the test. His testimony from that point on in his life was that he never had a need that wasn't met before he had it. His reluctant but complete obedience had unlocked for him a place in the spirit realm that he lived from for the rest of his days. His future was changed and altered because of his willingness to obey God. How we handle our finances does determine the future we have in this life, but also the one to come.

May I bring one more thought concerning this realm of prosperity that God has for us? We know that Abel gave a great offering and sacrifice that was pleasing to the Lord. Hebrews 11:4 shows that Abel's excellent sacrifice is having eternal consequences in his life even now.

> *By faith Abel offered to God a more excellent sacrifice than Cain, through which he obtained witness that he was righteous, God testifying of his gifts; and through it he being dead still speaks.*

Abel, in a heavenly dimension, is still speaking today. Even though he is dead from a natural standpoint, there are eternal results that stem from his extravagant offering. His offering was so excellent that God's testimony is speaking for him in heaven in the Courts. Our offerings that we bring, the way we handle our finances and generosity, will unlock for us not just an earthly future but a heavenly/eternal one as well. When we begin to recognize this, we see why the devil would want to hinder our prosperity legally. If we can undo these covenants with demons through repentance, renouncing, and giving back what has been claimed against us, we will see prosperity on new levels become our portion.

A sixth thing that the devil can claim against us is shame and degradation. If we don't fully revoke covenants with demons through giving back what they claimed we gained, shame can be our lot. Hosea 2:10-11 reveals the rights to bring these places of uncovering.

> *Now I will uncover her lewdness in the sight of her lovers,*
> *And no one shall deliver her from My hand.*
> *I will also cause all her mirth to cease,*
> *Her feast days,*

Her New Moons,
Her Sabbaths—
All her appointed feasts.

Notice that because of the unwillingness to give back and therefore undo trades completely, joy is replaced by shame and unveilings. Our God is a God who covers. It is not His desire to expose. He actually covers our shamefulness, giving us space and time to repent. Proverbs 10:12 let us know that love covers all sin. We know that God is love. Therefore it is His nature and desire to cover us and our sins.

Hatred stirs up strife,
But love covers all sins.

It is people who actually bring exposure through hatred. First Peter 4:8 amplifies this idea. We are to always walk in love to cover others' sins because this is the nature of God.

And above all things have fervent love for one another, for "love will cover a multitude of sins."

People of love and God Himself get no pleasure from the exposure of sin and shame. God loves to give even the most vile people the chance to repent. He even said this to Jezebel in Revelation 2:20-22.

Nevertheless I have a few things against you, because you allow that woman Jezebel, who calls herself a prophetess, to teach and seduce My servants to commit sexual immorality and eat things sacrificed to idols. And I gave her time to repent of her sexual immorality, and she did not

> *repent. Indeed I will cast her into a sickbed, and those who commit adultery with her into great tribulation, unless they repent of their deeds.*

Notice that God is still granting this person the opportunity to repent. He says He has given her time to repent. He is declaring that because she will not repent, judgment is coming. But then He says, "I'll do this *unless* they repent." Wow! God is still offering time to repent. This is because He doesn't want to expose. He only exposes for the sake of redemption when there is a soul at stake who is losing their eternity. We see Paul speaking of this in 1 Corinthians 5:4-5 concerning the man who is committing sexual sin with his stepmother. Paul is exposing this for the sake of this man's salvation.

> *In the name of our Lord Jesus Christ, when you are gathered together, along with my spirit, with the power of our Lord Jesus Christ, deliver such a one to Satan for the destruction of the flesh, that his spirit may be saved in the day of the Lord Jesus.*

Paul was declaring that this man, who was clearly in the church, was in danger of losing his salvation because of this immoral sin. The future consequences demanded an unveiling for redemptive purposes. This is the reason why God exposes. It is always to bring people to repentance who otherwise were resisting it. We also see Paul instructing Timothy in 1 Timothy 5:19-20 to deal with leaders who are sinning. This for the benefit of all others.

> *Do not receive an accusation against an elder except from two or three witnesses. Those who are sinning rebuke in the presence of all, that the rest also may fear.*

Notice that the rebuking of an elder is only after there have been multiple accusations. If it is examined and found to be a true problem, then elders are to be rebuked publicly. This is to restore the fear of the Lord to the people of God. Again, it is always for redemptive purposes and never for punishment. This is not the heart of our God.

However, the devil is one who loves to shame, expose, and ridicule. He desires to destroy reputations in order to diminish realms of influence. With his demonic powers, he can discover a legal right to do this if there are covenants in the bloodline. He will use this to legally shame us and diminish our places of impact and influence. Yet it is God who wants us to spread out in our influence to advance His kingdom. Isaiah 54:2-3 gives us insight into God's passion for us to influence on greater and greater levels.

> *Enlarge the place of your tent,*
> *And let them stretch out the curtains of your dwellings;*
> *Do not spare;*
> *Lengthen your cords,*
> *And strengthen your stakes.*
> *For you shall expand to the right and to the left,*
> *And your descendants will inherit the nations,*
> *And make the desolate cities inhabited.*

When we are told to enlarge our place, this is about influence and impact. Notice that the enlargement is about reclaiming nations and cities. Those who have become desolate are being redeemed and recovered with divine purpose. This is because our increased influence is allowing this to happen.

One of the things I have endured as a minister is great resistance and ridicule. This is not from people at large, but from those who it seemed were jealous of me and afraid of me. They have aggressively fought against my increase of influence. Yet the way God increases the rule of His kingdom in the earth is through giving us greater places of empowerment. Years ago, when I was in a very intense time with the Lord, I heard Him say to me, "I will make your name as one of the great men of the earth." I didn't ask to hear this. I wasn't trying to hear anything like this. I just heard it from the Lord. This word has been tested and fought for in the Courts of Heaven. I have had to undo demonic covenants that have claimed the legal right to shame and diminish my place of influence rather than see the promotion of the Lord. It is an ongoing battle to see what God has promised and desired be a reality. However, I know that as the rights to shame and diminish are removed, there will be a complete fulfillment of the word the Lord spoke. His word does not return void, and every spirit designed to hinder the fulfillment will be judged as illegal and unrighteous.

The seventh thing a demonic covenant that hasn't been completely undone can do is allow demonic activity. Hosea 2:12 declares that at one time there was the fruitfulness of God, but there is now a *beast* roaming and at work.

> *And I will destroy her vines and her fig trees,*
> *Of which she has said,*
> *"These are my wages that my lovers have given me."*
> *So I will make them a forest,*
> *And the beasts of the field shall eat them.*

"Beast" speak of demonic activity against us and the purposes of God. Notice that the vines and fig trees were taken over by the forest. In other words, it became covered and overgrown because it was no longer cultivated. It then became a place of beasts, which speaks of demons and devils operating. Revelation 13:1-2 calls the demonic entity that arises to be a part of ruling mankind a *beast.*

> *Then I stood on the sand of the sea. And I saw a beast rising up out of the sea, having seven heads and ten horns, and on his horns ten crowns, and on his heads a blasphemous name. Now the beast which I saw was like a leopard, his feet were like the feet of a bear, and his mouth like the mouth of a lion. The dragon gave him his power, his throne, and great authority.*

Notice that the very epitome of evil is called a *beast.* Of course Peter said that satan himself would function as a lion going forth to devour. We see this in 1 Peter 5:8. Demon powers are beasts that are here to devour and consume

> *Be sober, be vigilant; because your adversary the devil walks about like a roaring lion, seeking whom he may devour.*

This is the purpose of beasts and powers of darkness. When we read of beasts in the scriptures, we are reading of demon powers that will consume and devour if they are allowed.

It is the lack of cultivation and spiritual activity that can allow these beasts to operate. When there is holiness being pursued and cultivated, there will be no devouring beasts that can function. Isaiah 35:8-9 gives us the promise that as we walk in holiness, there will be no place for ravenous beasts.

> *A highway shall be there, and a road,*
> *And it shall be called the Highway of Holiness.*
> *The unclean shall not pass over it,*

But it shall be for others.
Whoever walks the road, although a fool,
Shall not go astray.
No lion shall be there,
Nor shall any ravenous beast go up on it;
It shall not be found there.
But the redeemed shall walk there.

On this *Highway of Holiness,* no lions, no consuming beasts, and no powers of darkness will be upon it. The holiness cultivated will not allow these powers against us to prosper. This is why we are told in 2 Corinthians 7:1 to *perfect* holiness in the fear of God. This renounces the powers of darkness from operating against us or even being close to us.

> *Therefore, having these promises, beloved, let us cleanse ourselves from all filthiness of the flesh and spirit, perfecting holiness in the fear of God.*

There are promises we cannot obtain and walk in unless we come to progressive holiness. This requires us cultivating our lives. When we do not spend time cultivating spiritual growth and postures, we make room for demons to operate. This is usually the result of laziness in our spiritual pursuits. In Proverbs 24:30-31, we see the result of laziness on any level. When we are lazy, walls get broken down and things get overgrown.

I went by the field of the lazy man,
And by the vineyard of the man devoid of understanding;
And there it was, all overgrown with thorns;

Its surface was covered with nettles;
Its stone wall was broken down.

Walls being broken down speaks of protections and resistances falling. Forces against us now have free rein to attack and destroy. This is what the Lord is declaring will have legal rights to us when we don't fully undo covenants with demons. Our lives and families can be afflicted with demon powers. This is why we are urged in Hebrews 6:11-12 to not be spiritually slothful. This will grant the devil legal rights as our spiritual lives become overgrown. We can end up becoming a forest when we were at one time a cultivated field.

And we desire that each one of you show the same diligence to the full assurance of hope until the end, that you do not become sluggish, but imitate those who through faith and patience inherit the promises.

Faith and patience are required to receive the promises God has for us. This means we must consistently operate in spiritual disciplines of prayer, the Word, fasting, and fellowship with the saints. If we practice these realms of cultivation, our lives will maintain a place of cultivation and spiritual wellbeing. However, if we stop cultivating our lives as the people of God, we make room for devils. This is why the *first job* of man in the earth was to cultivate and keep the Garden of Eden. Adam was given the job of keeping the Garden in Genesis 2:15. The Garden was a fruitful and obviously beautiful place. Yet it needed someone to take care of it.

Then the Lord God took the man and put him in the garden of Eden to tend and keep it.

God has always needed us to tend and keep our lives. The word *tend* means "to work" while the word *keep* means "to hedge in or create boundaries." We are to expend labor and always to create boundaries in our lives. Remember that Jesus in Matthew 11:28-30 didn't tell us we weren't to labor, but that our labor wouldn't be heavy.

> *Come to Me, all you who labor and are heavy laden, and I will give you rest. Take My yoke upon you and learn from Me, for I am gentle and lowly in heart, and you will find rest for your souls. For My yoke is easy and My burden is light.*

We are to work in agreement with the Lord. We are to maintain spiritual disciplines that allow the Lord's presence to occupy our lives. This will keep us from becoming overgrown and a place for the beasts of the fields. Creating right boundaries in our lives is also a necessary part of spiritual cultivation. Jesus told us in Matthew 7:13-14 that boundaries were necessary to entering into real life.

> *Enter by the narrow gate; for wide is the gate and broad is the way that leads to destruction, and there are many who go in by it. Because narrow is the gate and difficult is the way which leads to life, and there are few who find it.*

We cannot live unrestrained lives and expect to find the life Jesus promised us. The life Jesus promised us is a result of living under the mandates of His Lordship. When we subject ourselves to His authority in us and set the right boundaries in our life, we will know life as God longs for us to have it. This is a huge part of us cultivating our hearts before Him.

With all of this said, should there be covenants with demons in our bloodline, in spite of our well-intentioned efforts to cultivate our lives in fruitfulness, demons will claim a legal right to devour. We will witness this in our lives and our families. We must renounce all covenants and give back what demons claim we have gained. This is absolutely essential to undoing trades that created these covenants. Once these covenants are annulled, the demons of destruction will be removed from our lives.

If there was anything that I felt was taken care of in my spiritual walk, it was that I was one who had a cultivated place in God. I spent time in prayer every day. I read the word consistently and passionately. I walked in close communion with the Lord. Yet suddenly demons were consuming our lives. I couldn't figure out what was happening. I thought I must have committed some very grievous sin. What I didn't know was that I had become a bigger threat to the devil, and therefore he had commissioned a searching of my bloodline to find legal claims against me. This allowed him and his forces to attack and consume me in a ravenous way. More prayer wasn't going to solve the problem. This was what I thought was the solution to problems at this stage of my life. I could have prayed passionately 24 hours a day. This would not cure my situation. Only when I went into the Courts of Heaven and dealt with the legal issue that created the covenant in my bloodline with demon powers did the devouring stop.

The results were instantaneous. What all the praying had not accomplished, moments in the Courts of Heaven did. I'm not saying the immense time spent in prayer didn't affect this. It definitely gave me a history with God that allows quick results. However, only knowing how to approach God as Judge in His Courts produced the breakthrough I needed. So it will be for you as well, I believe. As we understand how to repent, renounce, and give back any and all the devil claims we have gained, all work against us will cease. The legal right to consume and devour will be removed, and we will see every ravenous thing lose its right to devour!

With all this said, here is a prayer to deal with any claim of the devil to do the four things we have mentioned in this chapter. These four results are what God's word says will happen if we claim the devil gave us something. Let's undo any right he claimed and give back what is allowing it.

> As I come before Your Courts, let it be recorded that I repent, renounce, and give back anything the devil claims I have gained from covenant with him. I am in covenant with Jesus through His body and blood that was given for me. I ask that any and every covenant that has been made with the devil in my bloodline now be revoked, annulled, dismantled, and removed from existence. I want nothing to do with the demonic realm and powers of darkness. I only want what is mine through my relationship with Jesus Christ!
>
> I therefore give back anything the demonic says I have gained through their influence. I declare that every good thing I have comes from my joining to Jesus. I only desire this in my life. As I give back whatever the realms of darkness say I gained, I ask that every trade that produced this covenant would no longer stand. Let the trade be annulled that is allowing these claims against me. My giving back what the demonic claims I gained, in finality undoes the trades that produced the covenants. As these covenants created through trades are

annulled, let any legal claim of the devil to destroy be removed. Let his rights to operate against me be revoked.

Let every hindrance and obstacle to me reaching my destiny, success, and future now be removed! Let every blessing I was made for now be set in place. I am free to come into the future and blessing of my God! Every legal claim based on anything the devil says he gave me is now revoked. I give back anything and everything they claim I gained. The trade made to create this covenant is now annulled.

I also say, let any claim against me to diminish my prosperity now be found illegal. As a result of covenants being annulled and anything gained being given back, let every right to afflict with lack, need, want, or poverty be revoked. I declare I am free to prosper and come into divine wealth. I will prosper and keep on prospering until I become very prosperous. I now have the power to get wealth and to enjoy good things, plus finance the kingdom of God by sowing into every good work.

As every covenant with demon powers is revoked and I give back anything they claim I have gained, let all shame designed to diminish influence now be removed. In the place of shame, let me arise and shine for my glory has now come. Let me come into realms of influence and impact that have been denied me. Let new places of influence be granted to me as one sent from You. Let Your kingdom advance because of these new places You are granting me.

As every covenant with demons is annulled through repentance, renouncing, and giving back anything claimed to have been gained, I ask that any and all demonic activity against me and my family be revoked and removed. Any devouring force, let it stop now in Jesus' Name. All harassments, sicknesses, troubles, marriage problems, financial issues, children in rebellion, and any other circumstance, let it now come to divine order in Jesus' Name! I declare that I am walking as one who diligently cultivates my relationship with Jesus. There is nothing overgrown. That which is cultivated does not become a forest. I am diligent and passionate in my pursuit of Jesus. Let any legal right the devil has claimed to consume though demonic effect now be found illegal and unrighteous. It must cease and desist in Jesus' Name. Every covenantal claim of the devil is now annulled and broken!

CHAPTER 11

INIQUITY UNDONE

Covenants with demons are one of the two main issues satan legally uses against us in our bloodline. The second issue is iniquity. Satan takes advantage of God's word to operate against us. Once we have dealt with covenants with demons in our bloodline, we must then deal with iniquitous issues that allow satan to claim legal rights against us.

This is what happened with me. Remember that I had been beset by delay and even denial of what I knew God had promised me. I was living a life of much frustration and bewilderment. Then I began to have an understanding of the Courts of Heaven. The first thing that was legally restraining me was a covenant with demons. However, there were going to be more things that I had to undo. In particular, iniquity in the bloodline was a problem. The word *iniquity* is one of four different kinds of trespasses against the Lord. Remember that these words are found in Psalm 32:1-2. This scripture gives us understanding of some of the legal issues that satan uses against us.

> *Blessed is he whose transgression is forgiven,*
> *Whose sin is covered.*
> *Blessed is the man to whom the Lord does not impute*

> *iniquity,*
> *And in whose spirit there is no deceit.*

These four—sin, transgression, deceit, and iniquity—are used by the devil to build cases against us. The word *iniquity* is sin that is in the bloodline or ancestral in nature. *Iniquity* in the Hebrew is the word *avon.* It means "a perversity, to be crooked." Ancestral sin can pervert who we are and fashion us into an image we were never meant to be. It creates within us a propensity/weakness for certain sins. We will look at this later in greater depth. With this limited understanding, we should know that satan uses iniquity as a legal claim to resist us and our generations. Exodus 20:4-5 gives us the legal precedence that the devil uses to visit the effect of iniquity upon a person and their family.

> *You shall not make for yourself a carved image—any likeness of anything that is in heaven above, or that is in the earth beneath, or that is in the water under the earth; you shall not bow down to them nor serve them. For I, the Lord your God, am a jealous God, visiting the iniquity of the fathers upon the children to the third and fourth generations of those who hate Me.*

This scripture gives the devil the right to affect generational lines for up to four generations. In other words, if there is an iniquitous sin that is practiced, then from that person, for up to four generations, satan can claim legal rights. This can be against a person or a family line. This would mean from the person who committed it, their children, grandchildren, great-grandchildren, and great-great-grandchildren could suffer the consequences of their sin. This would also mean that for me, the legal issues against me could come from my father, grandfather, great-grandfather, and great-great-grandfather.

Let me clarify some things here. When I first began to teach on the issues of bloodline cleansing, I taught that we should pray and open our bloodline up all the way to Adam and Eve. This was what was expressed to me when I first started functioning in the Courts of Heaven. However, even though I shared that idea, there was always something in the back of my mind that said this wasn't right. After all, God's standard in Exodus 20:4-5 was that the effects of iniquity in the bloodline could only be legally used for four generations at the most. I then thought about 1 Timothy 1:4, where Paul is instructing Timothy not to get caught up in endless genealogies.

> *Nor give heed to fables and endless genealogies, which cause disputes rather than godly edification which is in faith.*

The word *endless* is a Greek word that means *unfinished. Genealogies* means a "tracing by generations." We can derive from this that Paul is warning not to get caught up in something you can never finish. The searching out of our genealogies all the way back to Adam and Eve is an endless and fruitless effort. It gets us caught in something that can never be finished. This is why God set a *statute of limitations* on the effect of iniquity in the bloodline. It can only be legally used against us for no more than four generations.

This does at least two things. First of all, it makes cleansing our bloodline of iniquities possible. When something goes all the way back to Adam and Eve, it is impossible to get the work done. If it is only for four generations, then we can get accomplished what is necessary to revoke the rights of the devil to afflict us. This makes it feasible to see our bloodline cleansed of its iniquitous past. The second thing that this idea does is it keeps us from giving the devil opportunity he doesn't need. In other words, we don't let him present evidence in the Courts of Heaven past four generations against us. When I pray a prayer that says I open my bloodline up all the way to Adam and Eve, I have just made accessible to the devil things he should not have access to.

The fight in any court is about what is going to be allowed in as evidence. When we pray prayers that aren't in agreement with God's word, we can give satan privileges he doesn't need. If I say I am opening my bloodline for examination all the way to Adam and Eve, this gives the devil the right to use any of that to prosecute me. God said iniquity or bloodline sins could only be used from four generations behind me. When I saw this, this explained to me why I had a revelation about what was in my bloodline concerning iniquity. Remember that I had suffered delay and denial for 20 years. For this period of time, things would be promised me that would appear to be the means from which prophetic promises were going to be fulfilled. Then, what would seem to be the workings of the Lord on my behalf would be sabotaged in some way. All that was promised me was disregarded and dismissed. The person or people who promised the platform would renege and not fulfill what was said. This happened over and over again for 20 years. This definitely created in my heart a spirit of hope deferred that is spoken of in Proverbs 13:12.

> *Hope deferred makes the heart sick,*
> *But when the desire comes, it is a tree of life.*

I definitely had a sick heart that was full of skepticism and pessimism. I had become critical and judgmental as a result of all the broken promises that I had experienced. One occasion exemplifies it very well.

My daughter Sarah, who worked for me, called one day all excited. I had just written the book on *Operating in the Courts of Heaven.* It was doing really well as a self-published book. The reason it was self-published was because no real publisher would publish it. This was true of every book I had written. No bona fide publisher would give me a publishing agreement. This was another issue that plagued me. We had had some publishers agree to work with us, only to have them back out before a contract was signed. This was another problem in a long list of troubles working against us.

When Sarah called on this particular day, she was so excited. She began to tell me that a respected publisher wanted to talk with me about obtaining my book *Operating in the Courts of Heaven.* As she was excitedly relaying what the email had said, I was very nonchalant. I wasn't excited. The reason for this was I had been through it before and had nothing to show for it. Sarah began to tell me that she knew this was God. This was what we had been waiting for. This was what the Lord would use to give me a bigger platform for influence and ministry. I listened to her and simply said she should just respond to the email and say we were interested. She could tell I wasn't enthused at all. In her efforts to convince me that we were on the edge of the breakthrough we had been waiting for, she said these words, "Dad, I know this is God. I've always known you would change the world."

When these words were uttered by my daughter, conviction from the Spirit of God hit my heart. I suddenly realized my daughter had dreams for me I no longer had. I had a sick heart that had developed as a result of the years of disappointment and dashing of dreams. I was no longer able to dream anymore. This drove me to repentance and made me examine where I had come to in my heart. I began to ask the Lord to forgive me and cleanse me of my wounded heart and defiled spirit. I began asking that He would restore to me the ability to dream again and believe Him. This was to be critical to what was to happen next.

After this occurred, very quickly I had a dream that was to change my life. In this dream, there was a judgment against me from a court. The judgment against me was because my great-great-grandfather had done damage to someone through negligence. As I awoke from this dream I was in stark terror. I thought I was awakening to this being a natural reality. Maybe you have had one of these kinds of dreams. You wake up and think that what you've just dreamed is naturally true. This is what was going on with me. I was in complete fear. My throat was dry. I was convinced that this judgment against me because of what my great-great-grandfather had done was going to result in a lot of money to pay or even incarceration.

As I got fully awake, I began to realize this was *only* a dream. However, I very quickly began to know God was unveiling for me a truth about my ancestry. There was, in fact, a judgment against me. Only it wasn't in the natural court; it was in the heavenly court. The iniquity in my bloodline connected to my great-great-grandfather's sin of negligence was allowing the devil to prosecute me. Then I felt the Lord speak to me as I began to pray and repent for this iniquity in my bloodline. I heard the Lord say, "*Your great-great-grandfather through negligence stole the dreams of someone away; therefore, the enemy has claimed a legal right to steal your dreams away.*" Hence the years of disappointment and destruction of dreams. This was the reason why every opportunity and platform that seemed to be created was destroyed. It was because the devil was claiming a legal right based on the iniquity of my bloodline.

I got up that morning and immediately went to prayer. I remember repenting for myself for any place of negligence I had walked in. I repented of it generically for any place in my bloodline where this was operating. However, I zeroed in on my great-great-grandfather's sin of negligence against another person. As I prayed I began to feel the sorrow of repentance come over me. I asked that we might be forgiven for anything that had been done that destroyed the dreams of another person or family. I began to desire to make restitution for any loss that had been suffered. Of course, I didn't know any details of who had been wronged or what it was about. I could only repent from the knowledge I had been given. The desire was deeply there to bring restitution if possible. I believe this was because God was granting real repentance in this matter. I began to weep as I spoke before the Lord regarding what my ancestor had done. I prayed probably for about an hour until I felt that it was sufficiently dealt with in the Courts of Heaven. I had a witness that my repentance on behalf of my bloodline had been accepted. I was sure that the devil would no longer be able to use this sin against me and the future God had for me. I was right. We will look at the effects of this revelation and my response to it in the Courts of Heaven in the next chapters.

Let me lead us in a prayer before we move on to shut down any legal claim of the devil, in response to us opening our bloodline up back to Adam and Eve. We want to take away any place or opportunity we might inadvertently have given him.

> Lord, as I come before Your Courts, I repent for any place I have given the devil opportunity against me and my bloodline. Any time and any place where I have opened my bloodline up past four generations, I repent for. Any prayer I have

prayed that gave the devil access to my bloodline back to Adam and Eve, I repent and ask forgiveness for. I also call into place Your statute of limitations. Your word declares that iniquity is only allowed to affect three to four generations. I repent for concerning myself with endless genealogies. I come into agreement with Your word. Let any and all cases against me be dismissed that are based on anything past four generations. Let Your blood of sprinkling speak for me and silence all voices beyond these realms. Also, thank You that even the cases allowed against me from three and four generations of iniquity in my bloodline are now answered. Let me go free from any and every prosecution of the devil. Let me come into the success You have ordained for me. Let all delay now end in Jesus' Name, amen!

CHAPTER 12

INIQUITY: INTERRUPTION OF GOD'S WILL

As I began to deal with this particular iniquitous issue in my bloodline, I began to realize that iniquity not dealt with can have at least four different effects. Iniquity is a very negative thing. It has effects on us that we cannot realize unless our eyes are open to see it. We can be much more a product of iniquity in our bloodline than we can imagine. However, the Lord desires to free us from this power of iniquity and form us into His image and likeness.

I believe that there are two forces warring to fashion us. One is the Spirit of the Lord while the other is iniquity in our bloodline. One of these two will fashion us. The Holy Spirit moves in agreement with what is written in the books of heaven about us. We have spoken of the books that are in heaven in previous chapters. However, I would like to bring additional insight concerning these. As we have seen, David spoke of some of these books in Psalm 139:15-16. He actually said that his days and his substance were predestined and written in these books.

> *My frame was not hidden from You,*
> *When I was made in secret,*

And skillfully wrought in the lowest parts of the earth.
Your eyes saw my substance, being yet unformed.
And in Your book they all were written,
The days fashioned for me,
When as yet there were none of them.

My substance yet unformed speaks of my DNA. It speaks of the grace appointed to me before time began. Second Timothy 1:9 declares that purpose and grace were appointed and given to me before *time began.* This grace determines my gifting, my propensity, my attractions, and my desires.

Who has saved us and called us with a holy calling, not according to our works, but according to His own purpose and grace which was given to us in Christ Jesus before time began.

This is what determines the *substance* that God saw in me before I was formed. This substance or grace will drive me toward my purpose and empower me to fulfill it. This was written in a book in heaven about me. Also in this book, my days were written down before there were any of them. This means what I will accomplish and how long I will live. Basically David is revealing the same thing Paul spoke to Timothy about. David is calling *grace* substance and *days fashioned* is purpose. This is what the Holy Spirit is unveiling to us and strengthening us to fulfill. What is in our book from heaven is desiring to fashion and form us to satisfy God's passion through us. This is why Daniel 7:10 shows the Courts of Heaven seated and the books of heaven being opened.

A fiery stream issued
And came forth from before Him.

A thousand thousands ministered to Him;
Ten thousand times ten thousand stood before Him.
The court was seated,
And the books were opened.

We must know how to go before the Courts of Heaven and present cases from the books that are opened in heaven. In these books are our destinies and purposes. We can then in the Courts of Heaven get judgments that silence the voice of iniquity. Remember that iniquity is desiring to fashion us rather than what is written in the books of heaven.

Books being opened in the Courts is very important. If books are closed, we have no ability to perceive our prophetic destiny written in these books. Isaiah 29:10-12 shows us the tragedy of books being closed.

For the Lord has poured out on you
The spirit of deep sleep,
And has closed your eyes, namely, the prophets;
And He has covered your heads, namely, the seers.

The whole vision has become to you like the words of a book that is sealed, which men deliver to one who is literate, saying, "Read this, please."

And he says, "I cannot, for it is sealed."

Then the book is delivered to one who is illiterate, saying, "Read this, please."

And he says, "I am not literate."

This is an awesome revelation concerning how essential it is to have books open. Without books being opened, there is no revelation that can come. We are told that the prophets' eyes are closed and the heads of seers are covered. They have no ability to perceive prophetically what is happening. Then we are told *why* this is true. It is because the books are sealed. When the Bible speaks of literate and illiterate, it is speaking of those prophetically gifted and not gifted. Notice that neither have the ability to *read* what is in the book because of their sealed conditions. If books are sealed then people become frustrated. When books are sealed, prophets can prophesy the past or the present. However, they cannot prophesy the future. They can bring words about our past because it has happened and is known in the spirit world. They can bring words about our present circumstance because it is also known. However, to reveal issues about our future requires the books to be opened and prophetically discerned. This is where cases are presented from. The intent and desire of God for our lives is written in these books and must be prophetically discerned. If these books are sealed, there is frustration because there is no revelation concerning purpose. This is when Proverbs 29:18 can kicks in.

> *Where there is no revelation, the people cast off restraint;*
> *But happy is he who keeps the law.*

Prophetic revelation grants purpose to which we can give our lives. Without revelation, restraints are cast off, leading to a lust-filled life. We begin to live for the dictates of the flesh rather than the fulfilling of the purposes of God. It is essential that the books be opened and we discern our reason for being alive on the planet. This is what is to be fashioning and forming us.

We could speak of several issues to getting our books opened, should they be closed or sealed. However, let me mention what I consider to be the most important one. Worship will open our books. In Isaiah 29:11-13 we see why the books are closed in the first place.

> *The whole vision has become to you like the words of a book that is sealed, which men deliver to one who is literate, saying, "Read this, please."*
>
> *And he says, "I cannot, for it is sealed."*
>
> *Then the book is delivered to one who is illiterate, saying, "Read this, please."*
>
> *And he says, "I am not literate."*
>
> *Therefore the Lord said:*
>
> *"Inasmuch as these people draw near with their mouths*
> *And honor Me with their lips,*
> *But have removed their hearts far from Me,*
> *And their fear toward Me is taught by the commandment of men."*

Notice the reason there is no prophetic revelation from open books. This is because the books are closed. This is the result of no real worship. They are saying the right words but not from a heart of real worship. The result is no real drawing near to God with a heart of worship. The books are sealed and shut because of this. Think for just a moment about when the prophetic is released to people. In a service time in churches when real worship is entered into, people start getting prophetic revelation. They may desire to even speak the prophetic word they're hearing. This is because the worship is unlocking and opening books in the unseen realm. The prophetic people are then picking up and discerning the voice and heart of God. This is why Elisha called for a minstrel to play in 2 Kings 3:14-15.

And Elisha said, "As the Lord of hosts lives, before whom I stand, surely were it not that I regard the presence of Jehoshaphat king of Judah, I would not look at you, nor see you. But now bring me a musician."

Then it happened, when the musician played, that the hand of the Lord came upon him.

As they were desiring to hear the word of the Lord, Elisha knew a minstrel releasing a sound of worship to the Lord would open the heavenly realm. This would enable him as a prophet to discern the voice of the Lord. In essence, what was happening was the worship was opening books in the heavenly realm that Elisha could prophesy from. The truth is, if we desire to have our books opened and perceive prophetically what is in them, we should cultivate real worship. We can see three aspects of real worship that can open books. The wise men, seeking Jesus after His birth, were true worshipers. Herod, on the other hand, was a false one. The first aspect of true worshipers is they seek for the Lord. Seeking God will almost always involve inconvenience. This is a price we pay to find the One we desire to worship. It may involve rising early, staying up late, turning off the TV or social media or some other thing we enjoy. We have decided we want Jesus more than these other things. The sad truth is that quite often people would rather others do their seeking for them. Matthew 2:1-2 shows the wise men coming to worship Jesus. They are searching for Him. Real worshipers always have a heart to search for the One they desire to worship.

Now after Jesus was born in Bethlehem of Judea in the days of Herod the king, behold, wise men from the East came to Jerusalem, saying, "Where is He who has been

> *born King of the Jews? For we have seen His star in the East and have come to worship Him."*

They come to Herod thinking he would know of such a momentous event happening. They don't know that Herod is a wicked man who will seek to kill Jesus because he thinks He is a threat to his rule. Matthew 2:7-8 gives us insight into the difference between true worship and false worship.

> *Then Herod, when he had secretly called the wise men, determined from them what time the star appeared. And he sent them to Bethlehem and said, "Go and search carefully for the young Child, and when you have found Him, bring back word to me, that I may come and worship Him also."*

False worshipers always want someone else to do their seeking for them. Herod didn't desire to worship Jesus. These were just words in his mouth. A defining key to determine whether someone is a true worshiper is—are they seeking the One they desire to worship? These are the ones who have their books open. Their worship involves the seeking of Jesus with all their hearts. A second aspect to true worship is opening our treasures. In Matthew 2:11 we see these wise men as worshipers bringing their precious gifts.

> *And when they had come into the house, they saw the young Child with Mary His mother, and fell down and worshiped Him. And when they had opened their treasures, they presented gifts to Him: gold, frankincense, and myrrh.*

Their worship involved offerings of great wealth. Remember that we talked about our offerings and money having a voice in the Courts of Heaven. When we worship with financial gifts, it speaks for us in the Courts of Heaven. Prophetic understanding can unlock from the books in heaven as a result of this kind of extravagant worship. The third aspect of a real worshiper is that we hear from God. God warned the wise men in Matthew 2:12. This is what happens when people are real worshipers before the Lord.

> *Then, being divinely warned in a dream that they should not return to Herod, they departed for their own country another way.*

Their worship had brought them into remembrance before the Lord. God therefore spoke to them and warned them. This is the heritage of real worshipers. May we have this type of relationship with the Lord. He will esteem us because our worship has opened our books in heaven. Therefore, what is in the books is fashioning us for our future and destiny. However, iniquity is desiring to take us in another direction. Iniquity claims a legal right to fashion and form us because of what is in our bloodline. We must contend for what is written in our books to be the fashioning element of our lives. The truth is that when we stand before the Lord, we will be judged based on how much of our book we have accomplished. What was planned beforehand for us to fulfill will be our standard for judgment before His judgment seat. Second Corinthians 5:10-11 is a sobering scripture we must consider.

> *For we must all appear before the judgment seat of Christ, that each one may receive the things done in the body, according to what he has done, whether good or bad. Knowing, therefore, the terror of the Lord, we persuade men; but we are well known to God, and I also trust are well known in your consciences.*

We will be given rewards or suffer loss based on what we have done in our bodies. Our bodies are for the purpose of fulfilling what is written in our books, just as Jesus offered His body and fullfilled what was in His book. Hebrews 10:5-7 reveals this truth and idea.

> *Therefore, when He came into the world, He said:*
>
> *"Sacrifice and offering You did not desire,*
> *But a body You have prepared for Me.*
> *In burnt offerings and sacrifices for sin*
> *You had no pleasure.*
> *Then I said, 'Behold, I have come—*
> *In the volume of the book it is written of Me—*
> *To do Your will, O God.'"*

When I stand before the Lord, one of the things that will be part of my judgment is, did I in my body fulfill God's will and what was written in my book! If I am living my life to do the will of God written in my book, then my reward will be good. However, if I did other things than what was in my book, I will suffer loss. This is according to 1 Corinthians 3:13-15. How we build with our work determines whether we get a reward or not.

> *Each one's work will become clear; for the Day will declare it, because it will be revealed by fire; and the fire will test each one's work, of what sort it is. If anyone's work which he has built on it endures, he will receive a reward. If anyone's work is burned, he will suffer loss; but he himself will be saved, yet so as through fire.*

Whatever is written in my book will be works that produce a heavenly reward. If I gave myself to things not in my books, there will be loss suffered. Even if these were "good" works but not assigned by God. My greatest reward will be when I, from my body, fulfilled what was written about me in my books. My book in heaven will fashion and form me for my destiny and purpose if I move in agreement with it. It is my job to understand and satisfy all that is written in my book. Iniquity in my bloodline desires to take me in another direction. It will fashion me if I allow it. I must contend against any legal claim it is making in the Courts of Heaven. This is why Isaiah 43:26 tells us we are to judge with God anything that fights against what is in our books.

> *Put Me in remembrance;*
> *Let us contend together;*
> *State your case, that you may be acquitted.*

When we *put God in remembrance,* this is calling Him into remembrance concerning what He wrote in my book. I am reminding Him of my God-ordained future and destiny. I am taking the words from my book and rehearsing them before the Lord. This is critical, not because God doesn't know. It is critical because a judge can only render verdicts on the basis of evidence presented. Putting God in remembrance isn't about telling God something He doesn't know. It is about presenting a case that allows Him to rule in our favor. Without right evidence presented from the books of heaven, God cannot rule on our behalf.

We are then told that we are to *contend together.* This word *contend* is the Hebrew word *shaphat.* It means "to judge." God and us together are supposed to *judge* anything that fights against what we are calling God into remembrance about. Anything that is against what is in our books, we judge as illegal and unrighteous. This includes the iniquity of our bloodline. It will not fashion us. What is in our books will form us according to the word of the Lord. We have the right with God to render judgments. God and us together can and should judge anything fighting against what is in our books. This is the way we present cases before the Lord. We call Him into remembrance of what is in our books. Then we ask for and agree with God for judgment against anything that would be opposite of this. When we take up our authority and contend and judge these things, iniquity is destroyed and will not fashion our future. We are to be fashioned by the Lord. We are told in Romans 8:29 that we are preordained to be in the image of Jesus the Son.

> *For whom He foreknew, He also predestined to be conformed to the image of His Son, that He might be the firstborn among many brethren.*

God desires many sons to reflect the image and likeness of Jesus the Son. He is busily fashioning us into this likeness. Isaiah 43:1 speaks about God fashioning a people for Himself. There are some understandings we can glean concerning this process.

> *But now, thus says the Lord, who created you, O Jacob,*
> *And He who formed you, O Israel:*
> *"Fear not, for I have redeemed you;*
> *I have called you by your name;*
> *You are Mine."*

In this verse we see that God created, formed, redeemed, calls, and makes us His own. The word *create* means "to select and make." We are told in in the New Testament in Ephesians 1:4 that we were *chosen* by God before the foundations of the earth. God chose us and had a plan for us before time began.

> *Just as He chose us in Him before the foundation of the world, that we should be holy and without blame before Him in love.*

We are chosen to be accepted. We are accepted in the beloved with Him. After our selection, we are *formed.* This word in the Hebrew means to be "squeezed into shape, to press." As we are formed and fashioned by God, this is done through pressure. God uses the pressures of life to fashion us, if we know how to respond to them. It's not the pressures that shape us. It's the grace we obtain during the pressures and squeezing that shapes us. Pressures without the grace of God in our life only make us bitter. However, when we find the grace of God during these pressurized places, we can be fashioned into His image. This is why God told Paul during a squeezing time that His grace was sufficient for him. Second Corinthians 12:8-10 gives us insight into this process that we all go through.

> *Concerning this thing I pleaded with the Lord three times that it might depart from me. And He said to me, "My grace is sufficient for you, for My strength is made perfect in weakness." Therefore most gladly I will rather boast in my infirmities, that the power of Christ may rest upon me. Therefore I take pleasure in infirmities, in reproaches, in needs, in persecutions, in distresses, for Christ's sake. For when I am weak, then I am strong.*

In the midst of the difficulty, God was pouring grace into Paul's life. This grace Paul was receiving during this place of hardship would far outlast the hardship itself. It wasn't the hardship that was fashioning Paul. It was the grace being poured into his life that was forming him for his future now and in eternity. The grace certain people walk in is the result of what they received in very difficult times in their life. This is what has transformed them into who they are. They have met God in an unusual way and the resulting grace imparted has fashioned them.

Not only are we created and formed, we are also redeemed. This word in the Hebrew means "to buy back." The Lord is our redeemer. No matter how much we might have messed up or rebelled, God is our redeemer. He loves to make His love and graciousness apparent to all by manifesting His goodness in us. Ephesians 2:7 makes an amazing declaration about God's kindness and redemption toward us.

> *That in the ages to come He might show the exceeding riches of His grace in His kindness toward us in Christ Jesus.*

Notice that there are *ages* that we will transition into. We presently live in this age. We will transition into the next age at our death or the coming of the Lord. This is the age where we encounter heaven and its glory. However, there are ages after that. God is going to display in us the riches of His grace through His kindness. He will be displayed for the eternities of eternity as the great, kind, and good God He is. That will be made manifest in us. He is our redeemer. He bought us back by His sacrifice on the cross. Wow! What a God we serve.

The next thing God does is He *calls* us. This word *call* in the Hebrew means "to accost, to call out by name." If we *accost* someone, we are approaching them aggressively. We are confronting them. Sometimes we think the *call of God* is some kind of polite invitation. No way! The call of God is God accosting us and calling us out! We must respond to that call. I remember years ago when I had an encounter with God in my car as I was making a quick trip to the convenience store. It was around 1980. I was driving my 1973 Monte Carlo. I loved that car. I'm sure I was listening to the local rock and roll station. I would have been listening to the '70s music that wasn't the classics we know today. Then it was just the music of the hour. It was the music that I and my generation grew up on. In the midst of this, God suddenly entered my car. I sensed His presence clearly. I then heard these words: *"The time is drawing nigh for you to do My work."*

I knew it was the Lord. At this time in my life, I wasn't fully serving God. Other things had my interest. Mary and I had gotten married in 1977 straight out of high school. Two and a half years later, we had our first child we named Ryan. He was basically a newborn at this time. Now God was entering my car unannounced and accosting me. He was calling me out! As I heard His voice, I didn't want to do what He was telling me was my purpose to do. I responded to Him as I approached the stop sign in the road. I said, "*Why now, Lord?*" What I meant was, "I have responsibilities. I have a wife, a newborn son, a house payment, and everything else that goes with it."

As I asked this question, instantly God responded, *"Because now you have to trust Me."* The Lord was telling me He had me right where I needed to be. He was going to teach me how to walk in faith. This was God's call on my life. It interrupted my life. The call of God usually does. However, if we will allow the divine interruptions, God will do something amazing. He will prove Himself faithful to His word.

The other part of the process is God declares *you are Mine.* What a precious statement. We belong to the Lord. He will care for us and provide for us. We are His. In Zechariah 2:8 we see God proclaiming that we are the apple of His eye. This is known to mean the pupil in the eye.

> *For thus says the Lord of hosts: "He sent Me after glory, to the nations which plunder you; for he who touches you touches the apple of His eye."*

God declared that whoever touches those who belong to Him, they are actually sticking their finger in the eye of God. God will arise to vindicate and protect, because we are His. This is all because God has formed and fashioned us into what He desires us to be. However, iniquity wants to fashion us from our bloodline. Iniquity desires to disrupt the intentions of God in our lives. We must revoke its legal claim to turn us into the sin of our ancestry. Iniquity actually has the power to do the four distinct things in our life that I previously mentioned if we don't legally revoke its power. In the next chapter, we will see these four aspects of iniquity's influence.

> Lord, as we stand before Your Courts, we call You into remembrance of what You wrote in our book in heaven. We ask that what was written in our books will form and fashion us. Let Your divine will be done in us and through us. We ask for a judgment against all iniquity that would seek to fashion us instead. We say the iniquity in our bloodline is found to be illegal and unrighteous. It cannot form us or fashion us. We are here to fulfill what has been written in our books in heaven before the beginning of time. We submit

and surrender ourselves to this in Jesus' Name. We ask that there will be a full revelation of all that is written in our books in heaven. May they be opened and unveiled that we might prophetically understand and contend for everything in them to be fulfilled. Let Your Name, Lord, be glorified in all the earth, In Jesus' Name, amen.

CHAPTER 13

THE FOUR PURPOSES OF INIQUITY

Iniquity not dealt with will work powerfully against our lives, destiny, and future. Satan will use the legal rights that iniquity grants him to resist what God desires in our lives. Luke 22:31-32 shows that satan built a case against Peter. Jesus addressed this and declared that He had answered the case satan had brought.

> *And the Lord said, "Simon, Simon! Indeed, Satan has asked for you, that he may sift you as wheat. But I have prayed for you, that your faith should not fail; and when you have returned to Me, strengthen your brethren."*

The phrase *asked for you* in the Greek language means "to demand for trial." It is the word *exaiteomai.* Satan wasn't just requesting the right to attack Peter. He was literally demanding the right to put Peter on trial. Satan had an understanding of what the destiny of Peter would be. Satan wanted to alter this by bringing a case against him. He wanted to get something legal in place in the Courts of Heaven that would prohibit Peter from having the effect he was to have. However, Jesus stood on behalf of Peter.

When Jesus declared that He had prayed for Peter, He was saying He had answered the case against him. As a result of Jesus' activities in the Court of Heaven for Peter, the legal right of satan was silenced. Obviously, this didn't stop Peter from walking through some intense places of failure. He would deny the Lord and have to go through a place of God's gracious restoration. Yet when Jesus stood in the Courts of Heaven for Peter and won the case, Peter's destiny was assured and secured. He would fulfill what was set for him from the books of heaven.

We should know this is true for us, our loved ones, and any assignment God gives us to stand for people in the Courts of Heaven. Just because a verdict has been rendered for us doesn't mean we will not go through places of testing and trial. Just like Peter, we may walk through these. However, because of the verdict rendered, the legal claims of satan to deny us our destinies is revoked and annulled. We will walk out what God has arranged and declared for us to fulfill. The destiny has been secured because of the verdict from the Courts of Heaven.

I am sure that part of the case satan was bringing against Peter was from his bloodline. Probably Peter's impetuousness, arrogance, and other deficiencies in his character had roots in his bloodline. This is true for all of us. We are a product of what came before us. This can be good, but it can also be bad. The iniquity in our bloodline can form us rather than what is written in the books of heaven. What are the four effects of iniquity that fight against God's purpose in our life?

The first one is the *right to tempt us in a given area*. Iniquity not revoked legally out of our life allows the devil to bring temptation against us. Of course the devil is a tempter. There are two places in scripture where satan is called the *tempter.* The first one is in

Matthew 4:3 where the devil comes to Jesus and tempts Him to turn stones into bread.

> *Now when the tempter came to Him, he said, "If You are the Son of God, command that these stones become bread."*

We know that the devil tempted Jesus with three temptations in the wilderness. This is the first one. The scripture calls the devil the tempter. This is his nature and means of gaining legal rights against us. He deceptively tempts us; then when we give in, he builds a case against us because we have violated the word of God. It is a vicious cycle that we can find ourselves in if we yield to his temptation.

The other scripture where satan is called the temper is in 1 Thessalonians 3:5. Paul is concerned that these believers had surrendered to the tempter's temptation.

> *For this reason, when I could no longer endure it, I sent to know your faith, lest by some means the tempter had tempted you, and our labor might be in vain.*

Paul recognizes that the tempter had been successful in causing these believers to falter. What Paul had deposited in them could be lost. He knows that this is the chief means that satan uses. James 1:13-15 lets us know that the tempter uses what is in us to draw us away. In fact, this scripture is speaking of iniquity and its operation.

> *Let no one say when he is tempted, "I am tempted by God"; for God cannot be tempted by evil, nor does He Himself tempt anyone. But each one is tempted when he is drawn away by his own desires and enticed. Then,*

when desire has conceived, it gives birth to sin; and sin, when it is full-grown, brings forth death.

This scripture is giving us the full effect of iniquity operating unrestrained in our lives. First of all, God is not the tempter—the devil is. Notice that the temptation is about our own desires. Satan will entice us based on the iniquity that is in our lives. It can be a propensity for sexual lust, alcoholism, drug addictions, anger, or any other form of sin. We are told in this scripture that we are drawn away from God when we are enticed by the illegal desires in us. These desires are fashioned by the iniquity in the bloodline. The iniquity in the bloodline grants the devil the legal right to tempt us in a given area.

I learned this by looking at my own history. When I was just a boy of maybe three or four years old, we would get the Sears and Roebuck catalogue that would come to our house in the mail. This was a department store that carried anything and everything imaginable. I remember as a child loving to look in this catalogue. I would look in it at the toys and dream about what I might get at Christmas. However, I would do something else with this catalogue. I would take it and go behind a chair or into a secluded place and find the women in the catalogue in their underwear. I liked to look at the women in their underwear. Someone might condemn me for this, but this is just a fact about me.

Here's the question. Where does a three or four year old boy get the desire to look at women in their underwear? I had never been exposed to anything unclean or sexual. This was not a part of anything in our household. Where did this desire come from at such an early age? It came from the iniquity in my bloodline. Somewhere in my bloodline, there was sexual perversion practiced that gave the devil the legal right to tempt a small boy with this enticement. I am convinced that this is where strongholds come from in people's lives. The temptation of the devil based on iniquity in the bloodline allows strongholds to be built. Paul spoke of strongholds in 2 Corinthians 10:4.

> *For the weapons of our warfare are not carnal but mighty in God for pulling down strongholds.*

Strongholds can be overpowering desires to sin in a given area. They foster condemnation and guilt for the sincere believer. They seem to mock and ridicule those who love God and want to serve Him. One of the reasons why these things seem to be uncontrollable and overwhelming is because the root is iniquity in the bloodline. If we are to break these strongholds, we must deal with the iniquity that created the scenario for them to exist in the first place. When someone yields to the temptation that is empowered by the iniquity, these strongholds can be established. These are designed by the devil to control and dominate the lives of people. The beginning place of destroying these strongholds is to break their legal right to operate. Once the legal claim of the devil to bring temptation based on iniquity is removed, the desire to yield to this temptation will greatly lessen and even cease to exist.

The second effect of iniquity against the purposes of God is it *fashions our identity.* This is a humongous effect of iniquity, yet so unknown to most. In other words, iniquity forms what we think about ourselves. Identity is simply the innermost way we see ourselves. Iniquity will claim the right to form us into our past lineage's sin. It will claim that this is who we are based on iniquity's power. We see this happening to Isaiah in Isaiah 6:5-8. Isaiah is standing in the glory of God. In this place he sees himself as unworthy because of the sin and iniquity connected to him.

So I said:
"Woe is me, for I am undone!
Because I am a man of unclean lips,
And I dwell in the midst of a people of unclean lips;
For my eyes have seen the King,
The Lord of hosts."

Then one of the seraphim flew to me, having in his hand a live coal which he had taken with the tongs from the altar. And he touched my mouth with it, and said:

"Behold, this has touched your lips;
Your iniquity is taken away,
And your sin purged."
Also I heard the voice of the Lord, saying:
"Whom shall I send,
And who will go for Us?"
Then I said, "Here am I! Send me."

Isaiah's response as he stood in this place was "*Woe is me, for I am undone.*" The word *woe* is a lamentation or statement of great grief. The word *undone* means "to destroy or perish." Isaiah is effectively making the statement that he is so evil and unworthy that he should be destroyed. This is his present statement and persuasion of who he is. However, notice that the coal from the altar administered by the seraphim takes away the iniquity and purges his sin. Immediately, Isaiah goes from a sense of great guilt, shame, and unworthiness to a new identity. As he hears the Lord requesting who can go for them, he boldly volunteers to be the messenger. This is because in a moment, when his iniquity and sin is taken away, his whole identity changes. He begins to think completely differentlu about himself. Whereas as few moments before he was convinced of his uselessness, he now sees himself as worthy to be the mouthpiece of God. This is because his iniquity was taken away. It no longer had the power to alter the way Isaiah saw himself. He was free to be who God had made him to be.

This will happen for us as well. When we cleanse our bloodline and revoke the legal claim of iniquity against us, the inner idea of who we are changes. We can began to see and embrace who God has made us to be. We are no longer filled with shame and guilt. We are now empowered to walk out the destiny and future we were made for.

A third thing that iniquity does when it is not dealt with in our bloodline is it *destroys destinies*. Remember that iniquity fights against what is written in the books of heaven about us. If we agree with the iniquity in our bloodline, it can take us down a path of destruction rather than destiny. One of the issues in my bloodline was addiction. There is a history of alcoholism and drug addiction and all that is connected to it. Without seeking to uncover or shame, one of the best ways to expose this idea is from my own life. I have a twin brother. We were raised in the same conditions, by the same parents, and under the same influences. My parents came into the things of the Spirit when I was around twelve years old. We had been in a very legalistic church up until that time. We were part of that which got swept up in the Charismatic renewal and Jesus movement. As we began to be affected by this move of the Holy Spirit, I made one set of choices while my twin brother made another set. He became involved in the addictions that were in our bloodline. He ended up losing his marriage because of it. He also lost any contact with his children and grandchildren. He lived a life of sorrow and pain because of the addictions he let into his life. I say none of this with animosity or judgment toward him. In fact, I feel pity and remorse concerning this. He eventually died an early death because of the addictive control these substances had over his life. The iniquity in the bloodline that allowed this propensity toward addictions was never dealt with in his life. David actually spoke in Psalm 18:23 of not allowing ourselves to give in to these iniquitous compellings.

> *I was also blameless before Him,*
> *And I kept myself from my iniquity.*

David was aware that iniquity in the bloodline could put him in a weakened state to resist sin. Therefore, David purposely set a guard to keep himself from that which could destroy his life and future. I remember being in a meeting in a certain place. I was ministering with a prophet friend I had known for many years. As we were standing on the front row during worship, he leaned over to me. He spoke these words. He said, "The Lord just spoke to me about you."

I said, "What did He say?"

He said, "He told me that there were certain family curses that didn't get on you because you turned your heart to the Lord at an early age."

When he said this, I thought, *This is true.* This is why I went one direction, completely free from the addictions of my bloodline, while my brother got caught up in them. They were used to destroy his life, destiny, and future. They took him down a path of destruction rather than a path into his destiny. This was because of the choices he made as a result of the influence of iniquity in our bloodline. Because I gave my heart to the Lord at this early age, I had the power to resist the pull of iniquity from my bloodline.

I remember being in high school and being offered drugs and alcohol. There was an inner fear of God in me that caused me to say no when these were offered. I literally had a sense in the depth of my heart that if I never tried alcohol or drugs, then I would never have to face the temptation of doing them. This was my reasoning, even at this age and time of my life. As a result of this, I escaped the destruction from the iniquity in my bloodline that captured others. My prophet friend was right. Curses from my family never got on me because I turned my heart to the Lord at an early age. What had destructive consequences in others was never able to affect my life and destiny.

I have often wondered how many people who are homeless and living under bridges were designed by God to bring great breakthroughs to mankind? Their destinies were aborted. This is because the devil was able to legally use iniquity in their bloodline to alter their lives. We must know how to go into the Courts of Heaven, even on behalf of others, and free them from these devastating issues.

The fourth thing that iniquity does in our bloodline is it *allows cases to be built against us* in the Courts of Heaven. The devil claims legal rights and precedence to stop what is meant by God. We can see this when David had already been king for quite a while. Suddenly there was a famine and drought in the land of Israel. Second Samuel 21:1 shows us that this famine persisted for three years.

> *Now there was a famine in the days of David for three years, year after year; and David inquired of the Lord. And the Lord answered, "It is because of Saul and his bloodthirsty house, because he killed the Gibeonites."*

Perhaps in the first year, David didn't think much about the diminished harvest. Maybe in the second year he began to get a little concerned. When the third year rolled around and the famine continued, David began to realize this had a spiritual root connected to it. He asked the Lord why this was happening. God let him know it was because of a broken covenant with the Gibeonites. Saul had killed the Gibeonites Joshua had sworn to protect. This gave the devil a legal right to harass the nation of Israel with famine and drought. This famine occurred 70 years after what Saul had done. This was iniquity in the history of a nation. This broken covenant was allowing a famine to work against Israel and David's reign. David and the present Israel had done nothing wrong. Yet there was a legal claim coming from the history of this nation.

This covenant that had been broken was actually made under false pretenses. Remember that when Joshua and the armies of Israel came into the promised land, the Gibeonites deceived them. In Joshua 9:3-6 the Gibeonites are purposely seeking to save their own lives from the army of Israel. They have seen what Israel has done to every other inhabitant of the land. They devise this plan to trick Joshua and the leaders into making a covenant with them.

> *But when the inhabitants of Gibeon heard what Joshua had done to Jericho and Ai, they worked craftily, and went and pretended to be ambassadors. And they took old sacks on their donkeys, old wineskins torn and mended, old and patched sandals on their feet, and old garments on themselves; and all the bread of their provision was dry and moldy. And they went to Joshua, to the camp at Gilgal, and said to him and to the men of Israel, "We have come from a far country; now therefore, make a covenant with us."*

We know that because Joshua and the leaders did not seek the Lord about this first, they entered a covenant with Gibeon. Under trickery and false information, the leaders made an agreement in Joshua 9:14-18.

> *Then the men of Israel took some of their provisions; but they did not ask counsel of the Lord. So Joshua made peace with them, and made a covenant with them to let them live; and the rulers of the congregation swore to them.*
>
> *And it happened at the end of three days, after they had made a covenant with them, that they heard that they were their neighbors who dwelt near them. Then the children of Israel journeyed and came to their cities on the third day. Now their cities were Gibeon, Chephirah, Beeroth, and Kirjath Jearim. But the children of Israel did not attack them, because the rulers of the congregation had sworn to them by the Lord God of Israel. And all the congregation complained against the rulers.*

This is what had happened several hundred years before the famine in David's day. Yet the devil was claiming a legal right based on a deceptive covenant that was entered into. This would mean that if there is a broken covenant in our life or our bloodline, the devil can exploit this. He can visit our lives with famine, need, lack, and even poverty. Even if there was an unwise covenant made, it can be used by the devil to bring about limitations and restrictions. We must know how to go into the Courts of Heaven and remove the legal claims satan could be making.

I had this happen to me on a very personal level. I had a man on my staff when I raised up and led the work in Waco, Texas. He and his wife left to go to their next endeavor. What I didn't know was that this man behind the scenes had been doing me much harm. I had a dream after they left that he was a vampire sucking the lifeblood from the ministry. When I knew this prophetically and also through investigation after the fact, I determined I would not give him another cent of what I had promised. When they left the ministry, there was still a pay period for which he would have gotten a paycheck. I remember saying to him when they left that I would send him his last pay. Then I found out about the slander, attacks, and outright efforts to destroy that he had been involved in. I was furious and felt very justified in not sending him another dime from the ministry.

After several weeks, the ministry hit a financial problem. The offerings went down even though every other aspect seemed good. It continued to get worse and worse. I decided I was going to have to make some drastic changes or we were heading for serious financial trouble. I called the staff in on Thursday afternoon. I told them where we were and that unless there was a miracle in that week's offering I would have to lay several of them off. It was not a good time. We normally had Fridays off. So I went home that evening hoping and praying for a miracle.

As I woke up Friday morning, it seemed that the scripture we talked about in 1 Samuel 21 was staring me in the face. I had not thought about these verses. As I lay on my back in the early morning hours, the Lord told me that I had broken covenant and not kept my word to this man. I had promised him his paycheck. Just like Joshua had made an unwise covenant with the Gibeonites, so I had done with this man. It didn't matter what he had or had not done. There was a covenant in place. I had to fulfill my word and honor this covenant. The devil was using my broken word as a legal right to dry up the ministry's finances and put us in this terrible place.

I got out of bed and did one of the hardest things I ever had to do. I called the man and apologized for not honoring my word. I repented and told him the money was on the way. This was Friday morning. On Sunday, we had one of if not the biggest regular offering we ever had. The famine broke and no one lost their job. All because God gave me insight and the wisdom to repent for a broken covenant that was allowing the devil the legal right to devour.

We must know how to operate in the Courts of Heaven to annul the effects of iniquity that would work against the purposes of God. Satan uses iniquity and sin from our history as a legal claim against us. Even though this was my own personal fault, the principle of broken covenants in our bloodline can be exploited. We must repent for ourselves and bloodline issues to revoke iniquity's rights.

> As I stand in Your Courts, Lord, I repent for myself and my bloodline. I ask that any sin in my history would now be answered by the precious blood of sprinkling that speaks on my behalf. As I repent for iniquity, let any legal claim the devil is using against me be annulled. Do not allow him to speak against me in Your Courts. Revoke and silence every legal argument against me based on the iniquity of my forefathers, in Jesus' Name.
>
> As I stand before You, Lord, I ask that any and all effects of iniquity against Your purposes in my life be removed. Let any and every right to tempt me in a given area be revoked. Let the power of iniquity to trap and bring me captive be renounced and removed now. Let any effect of iniquity in my life to fashion my identity be removed. Let my

spirit, soul, and mind go free to think the way You would have me think about myself. Do not let the iniquity in my history fashion the way I see myself, in Jesus' Name.

I also ask that iniquity would not have power over me. As David declared, let me keep myself from iniquity. Let not iniquity cause me to make choices that thwart my destiny. Deliver me from destruction and bring me into my destiny and future, in Jesus' Name.

I also ask, any legal claim satan is making against me to build a case, may it be annulled and silenced. Let me go free from any and all legal accusations that result in a case to keep me from my God-ordained purpose. Let every restriction and limitation be revoked. Cause any and all covenant breaking to be set aside. I repent for any place in my life or my bloodline where there has been covenant breaking or the breaking our word. Forgive us, Lord, for this in Jesus' Name.

I ask, Lord, that You silence all right of iniquity to speak against me. Let its voice not be heard in Your Courts against me, in Jesus' Name, amen.

CHAPTER 14

SILENCING VOICES

One of the main things I have discovered is how to target voices in the spirit realm. I believe that voices are our chief opponent in the Courts of Heaven. If we can silence these voices, our breakthrough and victories can come quickly. If we are to understand this idea, let's revisit Revelation 12:10-11. This gives us great insight into what is happening in the unseen realm. This helps us be more proficient in our operation to cleanse our bloodlines in the Courts of Heaven.

> *Then I heard a loud voice saying in heaven, "Now salvation, and strength, and the kingdom of our God, and the power of His Christ have come, for the accuser of our brethren, who accused them before our God day and night, has been cast down. And they overcame him by the blood of the Lamb and by the word of their testimony, and they did not love their lives to the death."*

Please be reminded that the word *accuser* is the Greek word *katagoros*. It means "a complainant at law." Many believe that this is speaking of a natural person who decides they don't like us. This is not true. There are three reasons we can conclude this. First of all, notice that when the accuser/*katagoros* is cast down, there is a full manifestation of the kingdom of God. This is what it means when it says salvation, the kingdom of God, and the power of His Christ have come. We are told this happens *for the accuser is cast down*. It is the legal accusations of satan and the accuser that stop the fullness of breakthrough from happening. When the mouth and words of the accuser are silenced, the fullness of God can be manifested.

Notice also that the declaration being made is that *"now"* this has happened. I take this to mean it is now available to us. We aren't waiting for something else to occur. What needed to occur has taken place. If we are to get the full benefits of what is "*now*" available, we must set in place the judgments of God against the accuser. This is why we overcome by the blood of Lamb. It is our faith and operation as God's covenant people, in putting into place the testimony of the blood, that causes the accuser's voice to be silenced. Even though Jesus' work on the cross legally caused the devil to be cast down, we have to claim that legal work. We have to take the blood and present a case in the Courts of Heaven. The way I do this is I remind the Courts of what Jesus did by shedding His blood. I agree with the testimony of the blood on my behalf that is silencing any and every voice against me. I have discovered that if I can silence the myriad of voices in the spirit world against me, I can get breakthrough.

The second reason that it is apparent the accuser is in the legal realms of the spirit and not someone naturally speaking words against me is the accusations and complaints are being spoken to God. If it was a natural person, they don't talk to God—they talk to other people. That means the accuser of the brethren is talking against us in law before God. The third reason this is clearly a demonic assault and not from natural people is the accusation is day and night. In other words, it is perpetual. I've often said that

I might be bad but not bad enough to warrant nonstop words against my own actions and activities. Where would the devil get enough accusations to bring perpetual words against us? It would have to be our own actions, but also the history in our bloodline. This is why it is day and night. Satan is constantly presenting cases against us before the Courts of Heaven. I have found it is the voices that we need to silence. Isaiah 54:17 gives us insight and boldness to do this.

> *"No weapon formed against you shall prosper,*
> *And every tongue which rises against you in judgment*
> *You shall condemn.*
> *This is the heritage of the servants of the Lord,*
> *And their righteousness is from Me,"*
> *Says the Lord.*

Notice that it is the *tongue* rising against us in judgment that must be condemned. It is the tongue that is creating the weapon. We don't necessarily need to target the weapon. This can be a curse, a sickness, a hostile relationship, a financial catastrophe, or other troubles. We should realize these things can be a result of the tongues that are speaking against us. They are coming from the accuser of the brethren. The key is not to seek to undo the weapon. The key is to silence and condemn the voice/tongue that is allowing it to operate. The reason the weapon will not prosper is because we are condemning the tongues from the Courts of Heaven.

Notice that the tongue creates the judgment. The word *judgment* in the Hebrew language is *mishpat.* It means "a verdict or a sentence pronounced judicially." The voices in the unseen world can be determining the verdict or sentence I'm living under. If I can condemn this voice/tongue and silence it, my experience in life will change. The weapons will disappear because the tongue giving testimony against me is condemned and declared to be unrighteous and illegal. There are two things mentioned in this scripture that empower us to operate in the legal realms of heaven to accomplish this. First, we are told this is our heritage as servants of the Lord. This word *heritage* is the Hebrew word *nachalah*. It means "something inherited, an heirloom." It speaks of a birthright. When we are born again, we are granted a heritage from the Lord. We have authority to stand and undo words against us that would grant legal rights to land judgments. This is our heritage as the servants of the Lord. The word *servant* is the word for bondservant. In other words, our authority comes from being owned and possessed by the Lord. The more we are His, the more functional authority we can walk in to undo and silence words against us.

The other thing that grants us the authority to condemn words and voices against us as illegal and unrighteous is the righteousness of the Lord. We are told that *our righteousness from Him* allows us to condemn the tongues. As we have said before, it is righteousness in the spirit world that grants us authority. When we have the gift of righteousness by faith, we can silence every voice against us. We are commissioned by the Lord to reign in life according to Romans 5:17. The abundance of grace and the gift of righteousness grant us authority. This is why we can reign and overcome.

> *For if by the one man's offense death reigned through the one, much more those who receive abundance of grace and of the gift of righteousness will reign in life through the One, Jesus Christ.*

Death will not reign. We will reign because of the gifting of God in our life. This free gift of righteousness grants us the right to silence every word/tongue/voice against us. We no longer walk under condemnation and/or judgment. This position we are granted in the realms of heaven gives us the right and authority to silence the voices of the devil and of others.

This is essential to cleansing and reclaiming our bloodline. We can stand before the Lord in boldness and assurance. With confidence on the basis of Jesus' sacrifice for us and what it speaks in the Courts of Heaven, we can condemn the tongues of judgments. We can do this on behalf of our bloodline. When we condemn the tongue of accusation connected to our bloodlines, the devil loses the right to use it against us. We have requested and required that the blood of sprinkling speak for us. The testimony of Jesus' blood silences every other voice.

> As I stand before Your Courts, Lord, I ask that any and every voice speaking against me be silenced. Any weapon that has claimed legal right to bring any realm of destruction into my life, let it be revoked now in Jesus' Name. I remind the Courts as I stand in this place, that I am the bondservant of the Lord. I am yielded and surrendered to You. I also remind the Courts that I have placed my faith in Jesus and His righteousness for me. I received the gift of righteousness that grants me places of authority before You. From this place I ask and decree that any and every tongue be condemned. May these tongues be declared to be illegal and unrighteous. May they have no power to speak against me in Your Courts. May they

be silenced and every weapon dried up that they would empower! I thank You that this is granted from Your Courts in Jesus' Name, amen.

CHAPTER 15

SIGNS OF CURSES FROM OUR BLOODLINE

One of the main things people experience when there are cases against them from their bloodline is curses operating. Curses are spiritual forces that are allowed to sabotage our lives. They stop us from coming to success and fulfilling the purposes of God. We are told in Proverbs 26:2 that a curse cannot attach itself to us without a right or cause.

> *Like a flitting sparrow, like a flying swallow,*
> *So a curse without cause shall not alight.*

Curses are described here as birds looking for a place to land and put their feet down. This would say that there are spiritual forces examining our life, looking for legal rights to affect and bring ruin to us. The legal right is usually found in our bloodline. If we are to take away the legal right of a curse, we have to deal with the bloodline issues. Otherwise, curses will operate and bring ruin to us from our ancestral issues.

Let me give some insight into recognizing if there are curses that have claimed a legal right against us. Some of this understanding was gained because of what I walked through myself. I discovered truths about curses that helped me undo them from the Courts of Heaven. First of all, curses are designed to weaken us. This is why Balak, the King of Moab, asked Balaam to curse the children of Israel. In Numbers 22:6, we see the king desiring to see a curse operating against Israel so they can be defeated.

> *Therefore please come at once, curse this people for me, for they are too mighty for me. Perhaps I shall be able to defeat them and drive them out of the land, for I know that he whom you bless is blessed, and he whom you curse is cursed.*

Notice that the reason Balak desired Israel to be cursed was because he knew he couldn't defeat them without it working against them. This is the reason why satan desires curses to legally work against us. He knows without a curse against us we are unbeatable. Remember that 1 John 4:4 tells us that the greater One lives in us.

> *You are of God, little children, and have overcome them, because He who is in you is greater than he who is in the world.*

We are truly designed by God to be more than conquerors and overcomers. One of the ways the devil fights against this is by discovering legal rights to land curses from our bloodlines. Through these curses, we are weakened and made to be defeated. If we can see the legal claim of curses be annulled, we can see their power broken. This will allow us to operate in the strength of the greater One in our life.

Another sign of a curse is repetitive attacks. This was what initially convinced me of a curse operating against me. It seemed that we were suffering an onslaught on every side. It was as if all of hell had been unleashed against us. It was really likened to Isaiah 59:19. It was as if flood waters of demonic powers were suddenly coming from every side.

> *So shall they fear*
> *The name of the Lord from the west,*
> *And His glory from the rising of the sun;*
> *When the enemy comes in like a flood,*
> *The Spirit of the Lord will lift up a standard against him.*

The enemy coming in like a flood depicts an all-out attack of forces of darkness. David spoke of this in Psalm 18:4 when he described the attacks as a flood.

> *The pangs of death surrounded me,*
> *And the floods of ungodliness made me afraid.*

Notice that David talked about the fear associated with the floods of ungodliness against him. This is what seemed to happen with us. I had always been one who could endure. I would gird myself up and just fight and endure through anything that had come against us. Yet suddenly, before I could get through what was opposing us, something else would come. It kept piling on. Thing after thing piled on until it brought great weariness and fatigue. I then discovered it was the devil's discovering of bloodline issues that was allowing the unprecedented attack. Literally, in an instantaneous way, once the bloodline issues were legally revoked, all the attacks stopped. The floods dried up and the standard of the Lord was lifted against the enemy. The devil lost the legal right to bring attacks based on a curse he had legally landed.

Another sign of a curse is aggression. It will not stop until you stop it. Even though we have been delivered from the curse of the law, Deuteronomy 28:45 gives us understanding of how a curse operates. It is very aggressive and will come after you and all you love.

> *Moreover all these curses shall come upon you and pursue and overtake you, until you are destroyed, because you did not obey the voice of the Lord your God, to keep His commandments and His statutes which He commanded you.*

Notice that a curse comes upon us, pursues us, overtakes us, and destroys us. This means you can't outlast a curse. If it has legally found a right to land, it will not stop until you stop it. We see this in the days of Elisha when he broke the rights of the curse against Jericho. In 2 Kings 2:19 we find an otherwise very pleasant place to live operating under a curse. As soon as Elisha receives the mantle of Lord from Elijah, the men of the city petition him to undo the curse.

> *Then the men of the city said to Elisha, "Please notice, the situation of this city is pleasant, as my lord sees; but the water is bad, and the ground barren."*

The word *barren* is the Hebrew word *shakil.* It means "to miscarry and to bereave." This wasn't a matter of just some bad-tasting water. It was causing miscarriage, premature death, and bereavement. This was a result of the curse Joshua had set upon Jericho when it was destroyed several hundred years before. Joshua 6:26 rehearses this curse.

> *Then Joshua charged them at that time, saying, "Cursed be the man before the Lord who rises up and builds this city Jericho; he shall lay its foundation with his firstborn, and with his youngest he shall set up its gates."*

This was a curse of death and bereavement set upon Jericho. Even though it was a very pleasant place, this curse was bringing sorrow and pain. This is why the men of Jericho were pressing upon the newly anointed Elisha to undo the curse that Joshua had set into place. The Bible says that Elisha did as they desired. Second Kings 2:21-22 shows Elisha undoing the curse that had plagued this place for years.

> *Then he went out to the source of the water, and cast in the salt there, and said, "Thus says the Lord: 'I have healed this water; from it there shall be no more death or barrenness.'" So the water remains healed to this day, according to the word of Elisha which he spoke.*

Notice that he went to the source of the problem. The source of curses is usually in our bloodline. When we go to the source and undo the legal claim, the curse will end. Its aggression and pursuit of us will end and be no more. This is exactly what happened to me and my family. The aggressive attack stopped and ceased. It's legal claims to operate were removed.

One other thing that can be a sign of a curse is no prayer can seem to stop it. Again, this is what happened with us. I had always had a place of power with God in prayer. There wasn't anything that had come against us that I couldn't see defeated through persistent prayer. However, for about a three-year period it seemed that my prayers had no more power. Things were caving in on top of us, and I couldn't stop it. It was getting worse and worse with no hope in sight.

It was at this point that I discovered the Courts of Heaven. I was to later recognize that Jesus had put prayer in three dimensions in the book of Luke. He had spoken of approaching God as Father, Friend, and Judge. This is all revealed in my book by this name. However, I found out that when we approach God as Judge according to Luke 18:1-8, we step into a spiritual dimension called the Courts of Heaven. In this place, we can petition the Courts and the Judge and ask for legal verdicts. These verdicts will revoke the right of curse to operate against us. This is what I was discovering. When I found the Courts of Heaven and how to go before them, my prayers began to have greater effect than ever. Curses were annulled. Bloodline issues were erased. The rights of the devil as my legal opponent were revoked. Our lives began to come back to peace and blessing. Plus, the impact of our lives exponentially increased. All because the legal right for curses to operate was removed!

> Lord, as we stand before Your Courts we thank You that all You did on the cross has legally revoked the right of curses to operate. As I stand before You, may any legal claim in my life or from my bloodline be silenced that would give satan the right to land curses. I ask this Court that curses lose the right to come upon us, pursue us, overtake us, and/or destroy us. Let the curses looking for a legal right to land now be denied and dismissed.

May my life and family be freed from any place of cursing. May we walk in the blessing of the Lord and experience His goodness at every turn. In Jesus' Name, amen.

CHAPTER 16

THE CURSE OF PREMATURE DEATH

It is impossible to pinpoint every curse that can potentially land against our lives. However the Bible does give us insight into some curses and their causes that can afflict us. If there are iniquities or covenants with demons in our bloodline, they will allow curses to land against us. Let me list a few ideas for us to consider as we seek to undo the legal claim of curses to harass and bring destruction to our lives.

Innocent blood shed is a major reason why curses can land. This not only could involve murder but also would include abortions in our lives and/or bloodlines. Genesis 9:5-6 shows the standard of God that was set after the flood:

> *Surely for your lifeblood I will demand a reckoning; from the hand of every beast I will require it, and from the hand of man. From the hand of every man's brother I will require the life of man.*
>
> *"Whoever sheds man's blood,*
> *By man his blood shall be shed;*

For in the image of God
He made man."

The Lord said the "life" should be regarded as holy. It is to be respected, treasured, protected, and revered. If we are a party in any way to taking life away, this can result in a curse coming on us and our family. The shedding of innocent blood in our bloodline opens the legal door for the devil to land the curse of premature death against us. We are promised long and satisfying life in Psalm 91:16. We are told that if we set our love upon the Lord and serve Him, one of the benefits is long life.

With long life I will satisfy him,
And show him My salvation.

Not only will we live a long time on the earth, but we will experience the salvation of God during that time. When God shows us His salvation, it's not just speaking of that which is eternal. He is promising to protect, guard, and deliver us even in this life. We will live under the auspices of God's grace and goodness. Yet the devil is constantly looking for the legal right to land a curse of premature death to short-circuit this promise from God. If there is a shedding of innocent blood in our history and ancestry, it can allow this to occur.

I was teaching on this subject in a church setting a few years ago. After I finished the session, the pastor of the church came to me. He began to tell me that his family had been beset with the death of several of his siblings. He had watched as one by one his brothers and sisters had died prematurely. This pastor was only in his late 30s. It was clear that his siblings had died way before their time. He began to relate to me that after the last sibling had died prematurely, his grandmother came to him. She told him she needed to tell him a family secret no one knew. This discerning woman of God had a sense that it was connected to the ongoing death in their family line. She then confessed to this pastor that his grandfather had been in a bar fight years before. She told him that he had killed a man with a knife during that encounter. She told the pastor, her grandson, that she thought this was why the family had been ravished with premature death. The pastor then wisely prayed with this grandmother and repented for the activities of his grandfather. At that moment, something shifted in the spirit world. All premature death left the family line. The devil lost his legal right to visit this now godly family with death and despair. The right to bring destruction as a result of the shedding of innocent blood was ended!

Remember that this is *not* God doing this. The devil takes advantage of the standard of God's word that has been violated. On the basis of that violation, he requires the right to land curses. God loved this family. He didn't want the premature death of young people to bring the pain and suffering it did. Yet when the enemy brought cases against the people because of the shedding of innocent blood in the bloodline, the Lord could not stop the devil from doing this. This is what we have to see. Some want to blame God. Please remember that the Lord is good and kind and does not tempt with evil. It is the devil who takes advantage of what has occurred in the bloodline to land these curses. However, when we know how to repent and take the work of Jesus on the cross, we can answer any case against us and be free.

There are other reasons for premature death that can harass us as well. The Bible speaks of *sins unto death* in 1 John 5:16. This scripture is quite intriguing. Let's take a look:

> *If anyone sees his brother sinning a sin which does not lead to death, he will ask, and He will give him life for those who commit sin not leading to death. There is sin leading to death. I do not say that he should pray about that.*

This scripture could have a couple of possible meanings. One, it could be speaking of spiritual death. In other words, the Bible does tell us that it is possible for believers to lose their salvation. I know this is a subject with great contention attached to it. However, Hebrews 6:4-8 gives us understanding that we should consider. There are other scriptures as well that could be cited. This one, though, seems to say that it is possible to *lose* one's soul after we have been saved.

> *For it is impossible for those who were once enlightened, and have tasted the heavenly gift, and have become partakers of the Holy Spirit, and have tasted the good word of God and the powers of the age to come, if they fall away, to renew them again to repentance, since they crucify again for themselves the Son of God, and put Him to an open shame.*
>
> *For the earth which drinks in the rain that often comes upon it, and bears herbs useful for those by whom it is cultivated, receives blessing from God; but if it bears thorns and briers, it is rejected and near to being cursed, whose end is to be burned.*

Notice that there are five things that we as believers must have experienced to be able to fall away into perdition. We must have been *enlightened.* We must have *tasted the heavenly gift.* We must have been *partakers of the Holy Spirit.* We must have *tasted the good word of God.* We must have *tasted the powers of the age to come.* I don't have time to go into each of these in detail. However, only those who have had in-depth experiences and encounters with the Lord would qualify to lose their salvation. If I understand this scripture correctly, this makes it greatly improbable for most Christians today to fall into this category. However, this would be considered a sin unto death from a spiritual perspective. Yet I also believe that when John was writing about a *sin leading to death,* he was probably speaking about something that allowed physical premature death. I think if we are to walk in the wisdom of God, we should investigate what might allow the devil to visit us with premature death. What sin is there in us or our bloodline that would allow the curse of premature death to land. Let's look at some of these that can cause the curse of premature death to land.

The first thing I would additionally mention that can lead to premature death is taking the Lord's supper in an unworthy manner. First Corinthians 11:29-30 shows that some believers had died prematurely because they had in a nonchalant way taken communion.

> *For he who eats and drinks in an unworthy manner eats and drinks judgment to himself, not discerning the Lord's body. For this reason many are weak and sick among you, and many sleep.*

The cause for the premature death of some was not discerning the Lord's body. This can be two things. They were taking the Lord's supper through rote and routine. They did this instead of valuing through revelation what Jesus had done on the cross for them in His body and through His blood. This lack of reverence and discernment had resulted in weakness in the flesh. Some were also sick and others had died. This missing honor and worship for the Lord in the midst of communion did this. *Not discerning the Lord's body* also means that individual parts of the body were not being valued. Communion is not just the celebration of Jesus giving His body; it is also the valuing of the many-membered body of Christ. When we take communion, we are acknowledging this body as well, according to 1 Corinthians 10:16-17.

> *The cup of blessing which we bless, is it not the communion of the blood of Christ? The bread which we break, is it not the communion of the body of Christ? For we, though many, are one bread and one body; for we all partake of that one bread.*

Paul declares here that we are the one bread. We partake of each other as this one bread. When we do not discern properly the many-membered body of Christ, we are not valuing this expression of who He is. The result is a legal right of the devil to ultimately take us out prematurely. We must repent for this grievous sin personally and also in our bloodline. We want to remove any legal claim the devil would make to bring premature death.

There are eleven other instances when people died prematurely. I feel this is really important for us to examine, in that it can determine our lifespan. Let me just mention them, so we can take away any legal claims of the devil to land this curse.

Another thing that can cause premature death is the dishonor of the prophetic. Genesis 20:7 shows God warning Abimelech not to dishonor Abraham.

> *Now therefore, restore the man's wife; for he is a prophet, and he will pray for you and you shall live. But if you do*

> *not restore her, know that you shall surely die, you and all who are yours.*

Notice that if Abimelech didn't do what was being required of him to honor Abraham, he and *all of his would die.* The *all of his* spoke of his lineage. In other words, this sin of Abimelech could result in generational curses operating that created premature death in his lineage after him. Honoring the prophetic is a safe way to guard us and our generations.

Another thing that could incur premature death was a lack of reverence for God and not treating Him as holy. The priests had to honor God and His word. Otherwise, according to Exodus 28:43, they could die prematurely. I know we are not under the Levitical law. However, the devil is a legalist. We should know how to come before His Courts and disable any accusation the devil would bring against us.

> *They shall be on Aaron and on his sons when they come into the tabernacle of meeting, or when they come near the altar to minister in the holy place, that they do not incur iniquity and die. It shall be a statute forever to him and his descendants after him.*

This was about the prescribed garments the priests were to wear while in the presence of the Lord. We need to learn to treat the holy presence of the Lord as holy. Otherwise, we can suffer premature death. There are those right about now *screaming* at me that I'm a legalist bound by Old Testament law. However, in light of what I just said, we should remember Ananias and Sapphira. Remember the New Testament husband and wife team? They treated the presence of God as a common thing. They lied to God, the Holy Spirit, and the apostles. The result in Acts 5:1-11 was premature death. They wanted to make out like they were making as big a sacrifice as others were making. Others were selling land and bringing it all and giving it to God. They also sold possessions and made out like they were doing this as well. Their actions brought a judgment of premature death on them.

> *But a certain man named Ananias, with Sapphira his wife, sold a possession. And he kept back part of the proceeds, his wife also being aware of it, and brought a certain part and laid it at the apostles' feet. But Peter said, "Ananias, why has Satan filled your heart to lie to the Holy Spirit and keep back part of the price of the land for yourself? While it remained, was it not your own? And after it was sold, was it not in your own control? Why have you conceived this thing in your heart? You have not lied to men but to God."*
>
> *Then Ananias, hearing these words, fell down and breathed his last. So great fear came upon all those who heard these things. And the young men arose and wrapped him up, carried him out, and buried him.*
>
> *Now it was about three hours later when his wife came in, not knowing what had happened. And Peter answered her, "Tell me whether you sold the land for so much?"*
>
> *She said, "Yes, for so much."*
>
> *Then Peter said to her, "How is it that you have agreed together to test the Spirit of the Lord? Look, the feet of those who have buried your husband are at the door, and they will carry you out." Then immediately she fell down at his feet and breathed her last. And the young*

> *men came in and found her dead, and carrying her out, buried her by her husband. So great fear came upon all the church and upon all who heard these things.*

Treating God as holy and walking in the fear of the Lord is essential, whether it's the Old or New Testament. If we treat God as common, which is what it would mean to treat Him as unholy, we can grant the devil the legal right to visit us with premature death. We would be wise to operate in a holy mindset toward Him and His word.

Leviticus 10:1-3 shows Aaron's sons as priests losing their life prematurely. They offered up strange fire not commanded by the Lord.

> *Then Nadab and Abihu, the sons of Aaron, each took his censer and put fire in it, put incense on it, and offered profane fire before the Lord, which He had not commanded them. So fire went out from the Lord and devoured them, and they died before the Lord. And Moses said to Aaron, "This is what the Lord spoke, saying:*
>
> *'By those who come near Me*
> *I must be regarded as holy;*
> *And before all the people*
> *I must be glorified.'"*
>
> *So Aaron held his peace.*

These two sons of Aaron became presumptuous in their position as priests. The result was a judgment of the Lord against them that cost them their life. Again, remember that we are not saying God in this age is going to kill us. We are saying the devil will take a legal right connected to the violation of God's word to exact this punishment against us. He can, because of our sin, declare a legal right to land curses against us—one of which can be premature death.

What was the strange or profane fire that these guys set before the Lord? Some would contend that it was an unauthorized operation in the supernatural. In my estimation and opinion, this does happen today. People become so desirous of the supernatural realm that they step across lines and boundaries that are not to be crossed. This can shorten one's life. For instance, there are those who have learned the art of transporting themselves in the unseen world. They know how to teleport themselves in the spiritual realm. To illustrate this, let me tell you a real story that happened. There was a prophetic conference that was going on in a certain location. A speaker and his wife were at this conference. The wife woke up in the middle of the night and saw a man she was acquainted with hanging over their bed looking at them. When she saw him, she told him to get out. The man disappeared.

Let me be very clear. She physically saw this man, who had teleported into their room, looking at them. The next morning at breakfast, she saw this man. She went directly up to him and said, "What were you doing in our room last night?"

He denied and said, "I was not in your room."

She emphatically said back, "Yes, you were."

He continued to deny it, yet she wouldn't let him off the hook. He finally admitted he was there. She said to him, "Why were you there?"

He said, "I just wanted to see who you people are."

She looked at him with fierce determination and holy zeal and said, "If you ever do that again, I will let it be known what you do, who you are, and bring shame and reproach on your life." He sheepishly agreed that he would never cross that threshold again. She felt violated, exposed, and defamed by his activities. He had the ability to do this, but that didn't make it right. I have concluded that many of those who can produce this phenomenon have a history in witchcraft before they were saved. They draw from this history and the skills they obtained to still function in this realm. This is different from the Spirit of the Lord picking Philip up and transporting him to another place in Acts 8:39-40. This was the Holy Spirit's work, not something learned from witches and witchcraft.

> *Now when they came up out of the water, the Spirit of the Lord caught Philip away, so that the eunuch saw him no more; and he went on his way rejoicing. But Philip was found at Azotus. And passing through, he preached in all the cities till he came to Caesarea.*

I am fine with the Holy Spirit doing this to accomplish the purposes of God. However, when it is simply something novel that some have learned to do, this is another thing. This can be similar to profane or strange fire. If in fact this is a witchcraft ability, it will give the devil a legal right to end one's life prematurely. This connecting with the demonic is a very serious thing. We need to be very careful and make sure we are always following the leadership of the Holy Spirit in matters of the supernatural.

Another is when Uzzah was judged for touching the ark when it shook on the threshing floor in 2 Samuel 6:5-7. David had purposed to bring the ark of the covenant back to Jerusalem. It had been in captivity for many decades. David's passion for God's presence drove him to desire this ark back in his kingdom. The problem was, instead of bringing it up on the shoulders of the priests as described by God, he used a cart and some oxen. When they came to the threshing floor, the oxen stumbled and the ark shook on the cart.

> *Then David and all the house of Israel played music before the Lord on all kinds of instruments of fir wood, on harps, on stringed instruments, on tambourines, on sistrums, and on cymbals.*
>
> *And when they came to Nachon's threshing floor, Uzzah put out his hand to the ark of God and took hold of it, for the oxen stumbled. Then the anger of the Lord was aroused against Uzzah, and God struck him there for his error; and he died there by the ark of God.*

It appears Uzzah was simply trying to keep the ark from falling off the cart. The thing that allowed Uzzah to be killed was his presumption. Presumption before the Lord is a very dangerous thing. The ark of the covenant had been in the house of Abinadab from the time it was brought back out of captivity. In fact, according to 1 Samuel 7:1-2, it was there for twenty years.

> *Then the men of Kirjath Jearim came and took the ark of the Lord, and brought it into the house of Abinadab on the hill, and consecrated Eleazar his son to keep the ark of the Lord.*
>
> *So it was that the ark remained in Kirjath Jearim a long time; it was there twenty years. And all the house of Israel lamented after the Lord.*

Twenty years is a long time. This means the people in the house of Abinadab grew accustomed to the ark and its presence. When it came time for David to bring the ark back up to Jerusalem, the sons of Abinadab, Ahio and Uzzah, drove the ark. Second Samuel 6:3 gives us this piece of information.

> *So they set the ark of God on a new cart, and brought it out of the house of Abinadab, which was on the hill; and Uzzah and Ahio, the sons of Abinadab, drove the new cart.*

It seems that because Uzzah had been around the ark for twenty years, perhaps he had become very familiar with it. However, it was to be treated as holy and not common. His sin was that of presumption and familiarity. Presumption is connected to death. The sin of presumption will lead to us tempting the Lord, which can provoke Him. Numbers 14:11-12 shows that God in this provoked state was going to allow things that would cause the children of Israel's demise.

> *Then the Lord said to Moses: "How long will these people reject Me? And how long will they not believe Me, with all the signs which I have performed among them? I will strike them with the pestilence and disinherit them, and I will make of you a nation greater and mightier than they."*

Their unwillingness to believe and obey God was seen as a presumptuous thing before the Lord. As a result of them tempting and testing the Lord through their unbelief, God was sentencing them to death through a pestilence. However, Moses stood on their behalf and convinced God to not wipe them out. Numbers

14:19-23 shows us part of the conversation between Moses and God as he interceded for them.

> *"Pardon the iniquity of this people, I pray, according to the greatness of Your mercy, just as You have forgiven this people, from Egypt even until now."*
>
> *Then the Lord said: "I have pardoned, according to your word; but truly, as I live, all the earth shall be filled with the glory of the Lord— because all these men who have seen My glory and the signs which I did in Egypt and in the wilderness, and have put Me to the test now these ten times, and have not heeded My voice, they certainly shall not see the land of which I swore to their fathers, nor shall any of those who rejected Me see it."*

God pardoned the sin of the children of Israel yet said they would die in the wilderness because they had tested Him over and over. They presumed upon the Lord and tempted Him. This can lead to premature death. The devil can build a case against us because of our presumption. He can claim legal rights to remove us from the earth prematurely. May we repent for any and every place we have presumed upon the Lord. Another scripture makes this principle very clear. Deuteronomy 17:12-13 without reservation tells us that the sin of presumption will give permission to the devil to bring premature death.

> *Now the man who acts presumptuously and will not heed the priest who stands to minister there before the Lord your God, or the judge, that man shall die. So you shall put away the evil from Israel. And all the people shall hear and fear, and no longer act presumptuously.*

One last scripture that shows the rights granted the devil to land the curse of premature death is Deuteronomy 18:20. This is with regard to those who claim to be prophets and therefore speak presumptuously.

> *But the prophet who presumes to speak a word in My name, which I have not commanded him to speak, or who speaks in the name of other gods, that prophet shall die.*

I watch as different ones on social media make claims of prophetic authority or gifting. It concerns me greatly at times. If one is not what they say they are, this can grant legal rights to the devil to visit them and their generations with premature death. We need a new level of the fear of the Lord to come again to deliver us from presumption. Otherwise, satan can claim legal rights to bring death and destruction. It is the fear of the Lord that protects us from death and destruction. We can repent and turn our heart to the Lord and repent for any and all presumption. The devil's claims to bring death prematurely will be renounced and removed.

There are four more ideas in scripture that can lead to granting the curse of premature death the right to land. We will look at these in the next chapter so we can go before the Courts of Heaven and remove their right to operate. First, however, here is a prayer to undo these very important legal claims of the devil.

> Lord, as I stand before Your Courts, I humbly remind You that I am in covenant with You and Your purposes in the earth. My desire based on Your covenant promises is that I would live a long and satisfying life. I ask that any place I or anyone in my bloodline has given the devil legal

claim to thwart this promise would be revoked and rebuked. Let it be known that I repent for myself and my bloodline with regard to any and every place satan would claim legal right. I repent for any and all innocent bloodshed connected to us. Forgive me, Lord, any and all involvement in this horrendous thing. I repent for any dishonor or lack of fear in receiving communion or the Lord's supper. Forgive me, Lord, for not properly discerning the Lord's body. I repent, Lord, in Jesus' Name.

I also repent for any place I have not honored the prophets and/or the prophetic. I ask You to forgive and cleanse. Let it be known that I esteem and value Your prophetic word. I also repent for not treating You as holy, but treating You as common. You, Lord, are the holy God. May I walk in the fear of the Lord. Forgive any connection to strange fire in my life or my bloodline, in pursuit of the supernatural. I want only what comes from You.

I also repent for walking in presumption in any way. Any claim the devil is making against me because of presumption in me or my bloodline, I repent of this in Jesus' Name. I ask that this repentance might stand before You in Your Courts. Forgive me, Lord, for any and all of this. Let the devil's claims to shorten our life be revoked and removed. Thank You, Lord, for standing before us in the Courts of Heaven. In Jesus' Name, amen!

CHAPTER 17

REVOKING CURSES THAT SHORTEN LIFESPANS

When we began to look at this whole issue of premature death, it is quite amazing to see what scripture says about it. We have seen that the shedding of innocent blood in our bloodline can grant legal rights to the devil. He will claim this to visit untimely death on us and/or our lineage. We also looked at not receiving communion with reverence and understanding. We saw that dishonoring the prophetic can grant death in an untimely way. We've seen that treating God as holy and not common is very important to revoking legal claims of premature death. We saw that unintentionally or on-purpose partnering with demons to gain supernatural power can bring premature death. This is called strange or profane fire in the scriptures. We also became aware that presumption that tests the Lord can open us to premature death.

Again, please know that God is not doing any of this. It is the devil taking advantage of our own rebellion or rebellion in the bloodline to claim legal rights of destruction. However, if we go before the Courts of Heaven and remove these legal claims, we can gain the promise of God for a long and satisfying life. This is the inheritance for us as His covenant people. Let's look at the last four things that could give the enemy legal rights against us with regard to premature or untimely death.

In the event of Korah in Numbers 16:28-30, we see Moses saying if Korah and those with him died a normal, timely death, then they were not being judged by God. However, if they died a premature and untimely death in an unusual way, then it was the judgment of God.

> *And Moses said: "By this you shall know that the Lord has sent me to do all these works, for I have not done them of my own will. If these men die naturally like all men, or if they are visited by the common fate of all men, then the Lord has not sent me. But if the Lord creates a new thing, and the earth opens its mouth and swallows them up with all that belongs to them, and they go down alive into the pit, then you will understand that these men have rejected the Lord."*

The issue that caused Korah and those with him to die prematurely was rebellion against God's authority. Moses was the delegated authority of the Lord. Their rebellion gave the devil the legal right to kill them prematurely from a New Testament perspective. We are to walk in submission to delegated authority according to Romans 13:1-2. Otherwise, we can have cases against us to visit us with premature death.

> *Let every soul be subject to the governing authorities. For there is no authority except from God, and the authorities that exist are appointed by God. Therefore whoever resists*

> *the authority resists the ordinance of God, and those who resist will bring judgment on themselves.*

Submission to authority is submission unto God. Resistance to authority is resistance to God. This is what Korah and his company operated in. This gives the devil the right to build cases against us. We should ask the Lord to examine and judge our hearts that we not be guilty of such. We must repent for anything in our bloodline with regard to rebellion against authorities that represent God.

Proverbs 23:13 gives us a warning concerning our children and premature death. We are told that the correcting of our children will preserve them from the legal rights of the devil to take them out prematurely.

> *Do not withhold correction from a child,*
> *For if you beat him with a rod, he will not die.*

We are told that if we correct our children, they will not die. Our correcting of our children will remove from them the tendency to operate in a way that the devil can build cases against them. We are doing our children a tremendous favor when we lovingly correct them. We are protecting them from premature death. Please do not buy into the lie of wanting to be your child's friend, especially in their formative years. Your child doesn't need a friend; they need parents. When we correct them, we are securing for them a future free from premature death.

In my opinion, one of the biggest claims of the devil to shorten lifespans is the dishonor of father and mother. This is another thing that can bring the curse of a shortened life. When this is walked in, satan makes claims against us. Ephesians 6:1-3 is vehement about this idea and principle.

> *Children, obey your parents in the Lord, for this is right. "Honor your father and mother," which is the first commandment with promise: "that it may be well with you and you may live long on the earth."*

When we honor father and mother, we are securing a long life and success within that life. If there is dishonor toward our parents, satan builds cases to shorten our life. We must repent. Honoring father and mother is not just when we are growing up. Honoring father and mother is a lifetime issue. Even should they be dead, we are to have a heart and words of honor. Of course, there are those situations in which fathers and/or mothers were offensive, hurtful, abusive, or even sexual predators. I know it is hard, but we are to still honor them. Without honor, the devil will build a case against us to kill us. Some would ask, "How can this be done?" The answer is only by the grace of God and understanding the word of God. We see this in the life of Noah and his sons in Genesis 9:20-27.

> *And Noah began to be a farmer, and he planted a vineyard. Then he drank of the wine and was drunk, and became uncovered in his tent. And Ham, the father of Canaan, saw the nakedness of his father, and told his two brothers outside. But Shem and Japheth took a garment, laid it on both their shoulders, and went backward and covered the nakedness of their father. Their faces were turned away, and they did not see their father's nakedness.*
>
> *So Noah awoke from his wine, and knew what his younger son had done to him. Then he said:*

> *"Cursed be Canaan;*
> *A servant of servants*
> *He shall be to his brethren."*
>
> *And he said:*
>
> *"Blessed be the Lord,*
> *The God of Shem,*
> *And may Canaan be his servant.*
> *May God enlarge Japheth,*
> *And may he dwell in the tents of Shem;*
> *And may Canaan be his servant."*

If honor was about performance, Noah was not to be honored. However, the one who cursed and spoke evil of his father got cursed. He uncovered his father to his brothers. This resulted in not just a curse on him but on his lineage. Notice that Noah pronounced a curse on Canaan. Ham was the son who uncovered and dishonored authority. Noah proclaimed that his brothers would possess his inheritance. This is what happened when the children of Israel took possession of Canaan and the promised land. This was the result of the curse Noah had set on Ham when he dishonored the position of his father.

The ones who covered and blessed their father even in his failure got blessed. Even though his performance would have seemed to demand dishonor, his position required honor. The two older sons honored the position. This resulted in a blessing on them and their lineage. The younger who uncovered Noah got a curse on him and his lineage. We must honor parents for position even if we can't honor practice and performance. The fact is that without our parents, we wouldn't exist in the earth. Our existence is a result of them conceiving and parenting us. This alone demands honor toward them. When this is in place, we are promised long life and success.

The final thought on what can bring a shortened life and premature death is found in Ecclesiastes 7:17. We are told that much wickedness and foolishness can result in us dying early.

> *Do not be overly wicked,*
> *Nor be foolish:*
> *Why should you die before your time?*

This word *wicked* in the Hebrew is *rasha*. It means "hostile to God, guilty of sin against God or man, criminal, guilty one, one guilty of a crime."

Clearly this is speaking of a crime against God and man before the Courts of Heaven. We should learn to stand in the Courts of Heaven and persistently undo accusations against us that would allow early death to occur. We also see that being *foolish* can contribute to dying before our time. This word *foolish* in the Hebrew is *cakal*. It means to be silly. One of the characteristics of a foolish person is found in Ecclesiastes 10:14. We are told that a fool talks a lot.

> *A fool also multiplies words.*
> *No man knows what is to be;*
> *Who can tell him what will be after him?*

If we multiply our words, we are setting in motion the use of those words in the Courts of Heaven. I believe that being very measured in our speech is helpful in securing good outcomes from the Courts of Heaven. We are instructed in Matthew 12:36-37 to be aware of the judgments that can come on us from many words.

> *But I say to you that for every idle word men may speak, they will give account of it in the day of judgment. For by your words you will be justified, and by your words you will be condemned.*

Much foolishness is connected to many words being spoken without thought. The enemy can take these words and use them against us in the Courts of Heaven. Clearly according to what Jesus said, our words will be used to justify or condemn us. This is obviously in a judicial setting. We should repent for the words we have spoken or the words from our bloodline. This will help secure for us the blessing of a long life. The curse of premature death will be eradicated.

> As I stand before Your Courts, Lord, I repent for myself and my bloodline of all things that would grant the devil a legal right to land the curse of a shortened life. I desire the promise of God that I will live a long and satisfying life. I therefore repent for myself and my bloodline for all rebellion against God and His delegated authority. I ask that any claim satan is bringing against me be silenced by the speaking blood of Jesus on my behalf. I also repent for myself and my bloodline for any place we haven't disciplined our children in a righteous manner. Let any curse from our bloodline be revoked and removed that would let our children die prematurely. We choose to bring our children up in the admonition and nurture of the Lord. I also repent for all dishonor toward parents. Your word promises long life and success

when we honor parents. I choose to honor my parents as a result of their position if not for their performance. I let them go and forgive them of any insufficiency or inadequacy. I esteem them in my life. Let every curse associated with my life or bloodline connected to parental dishonor now be removed. I also repent for abundance of wickedness and foolishness in my life and/or bloodline. May this be dismissed before You. Don't allow the devil the right to claim a case to bring premature death. May I guard my mouth and speak right words so that I would not be esteemed as foolish. May any words from my ancestral past be revoked as well. Let every curse be lifted that could bring a shortened life or premature death. I claim a long and satisfying life for myself and my family, in Jesus' Name, amen.

CHAPTER 18

FROM DEFENDANT TO JUDGE

Once we have dealt with our bloodline issues, especially covenants with demons and iniquities, we can move from a defendant in the Courts of Heaven to operating as a judge! We see this in Zechariah 3:1-7. Joshua the high priest is found to have on filthy garments. This is because of iniquity. Remember that iniquity is the sin in our bloodline. The devil is using this against Joshua the high priest to keep him from his duties and call.

> *Then he showed me Joshua the high priest standing before the Angel of the Lord, and Satan standing at his right hand to oppose him. And the Lord said to Satan, "The Lord rebuke you, Satan! The Lord who has chosen Jerusalem rebuke you! Is this not a brand plucked from the fire?"*
>
> *Now Joshua was clothed with filthy garments, and was standing before the Angel.*
>
> *Then He answered and spoke to those who stood before Him, saying, "Take away the filthy garments from him."*

> *And to him He said, "See, I have removed your iniquity from you, and I will clothe you with rich robes."*
>
> *And I said, "Let them put a clean turban on his head."*
>
> *So they put a clean turban on his head, and they put the clothes on him. And the Angel of the Lord stood by.*
>
> *Then the Angel of the Lord admonished Joshua, saying, "Thus says the Lord of hosts:*
>
> *'If you will walk in My ways,*
> *And if you will keep My command,*
> *Then you shall also judge My house,*
> *And likewise have charge of My courts;*
> *I will give you places to walk*
> *Among these who stand here.'"*

The purpose of the high priest was to represent a culture/nation before the Lord. Through their legal work, there was a securing of the blessing of God upon Israel. The enemy was accusing and resisting Joshua the high priest from this function. He was a defendant in the Courts of Heaven because of the filthy garments he had on. These defiled garments were a result of the iniquity. We know this because of Zechariah 3:4. The cause of the uncleanness that is denying Joshua the right to function is iniquity.

> *Then He answered and spoke to those who stood before Him, saying, "Take away the filthy garments from him." And to him He said, "See, I have removed your iniquity from you, and I will clothe you with rich robes."*

Notice that as a result of removing iniquity or the sin in the bloodline, Joshua is clothed with clean garments. He is then given the right to walk in the heavenly dimension as a judge. He will judge the house and have charge of the courts. This is where God will ultimately take us. We will stop being defendants in the Courts of Heaven and become judges who can be a part of the judicial system of God. This will let us not only represent ourselves and our families in the Court of Heaven, but also the culture we are a part of. We will be able to secure from heaven the blessings of God for these cultures and nations. This is why we are called kings and priests to our God in Revelation 1:5-6.

> *And from Jesus Christ, the faithful witness, the firstborn from the dead, and the ruler over the kings of the earth.*
>
> *To Him who loved us and washed us from our sins in His own blood, and has made us kings and priests to His God and Father, to Him be glory and dominion forever and ever. Amen.*

Being washed in His blood makes us kings and priests. As priests we are positioned in the spirit world to present cases for the culture we are a part of. We as kings can then decree the blessings of God into place within our culture. This is all because the blood has washed us from our sins and iniquities. We are positioned not as defendants, but as judges in the Courts of Heaven. This position lets us be a part of the process of the Courts of Heaven. This is why Daniel saw thrones or seats set in place as a part of the Courts of Heaven. Daniel 7:9-10 shows us that the Courts of Heaven is a panel of judges with God as the chief Judge. He is the Ancient of Days.

> *I watched till thrones were put in place,*
> *And the Ancient of Days was seated;*
> *His garment was white as snow,*

And the hair of His head was like pure wool.
His throne was a fiery flame,
Its wheels a burning fire;
A fiery stream issued
And came forth from before Him.
A thousand thousands ministered to Him;
Ten thousand times ten thousand stood before Him.
The court was seated,
And the books were opened.

The thrones set into place are for those who have qualified to sit upon them. This is what Joshua the high priest did. When the unclean garments were removed, he was made a judge rather than a defendant. This is why he was told he could operate as a judge in the house and have charge of the judicial system. This is what judges do. It happened when he had the iniquity purged and removed. He was able to sit upon one of the thrones in the spirit realm as a part of the Courts of Heaven. So can we as well. When we deal with our bloodline issues, we are granted new seats of authority in the spirit world. We can take our place as a part of the Courts of Heaven and its process. My admonishment is to arise in boldness and take the place granted by God. Jesus' blood is sufficient to cleanse us and give us a place in our God's judicial order.

> Lord, as I stand before Your Courts, I thank You that Your blood speaks for me. I and my bloodline are cleansed from every defilement and legal word against me. I now move from defendant in the Courts of Heaven to the place as a judge. I take my seat that You would graciously grant me. May I from this place represent myself, my

family, and my culture before Your Courts. Thank You that You have granted me this place in Your judicial order. I am honored and grateful to You for Your grace that allows this. May Your Name be glorified as I stand in this place before You. To You alone belongs the glory and honor. In Jesus' Name, amen.

ABOUT ROBERT HENDERSON

Robert Henderson is a global apostolic leader who operates in revelation and impartation. His teaching empowers the body of Christ to see the hidden truths of Scripture clearly and apply them for breakthrough results. Driven by a mandate to disciple nations through writing and speaking, Robert travels extensively around the globe, teaching on the apostolic, the kingdom of God, the Seven Mountains, and most notably the Courts of Heaven. He has been married to Mary for 47 years. They have six children and nine grandchildren. Together they are enjoying life in beautiful Colorado Springs, Colorado.

In the Right Hands, This Book Will Change Lives!

Most of the people who need this message will not be looking for this book. To change their lives, you need to **put a copy of this book in their hands.**

Our ministry is constantly seeking methods to find the people who need this anointed message to change their lives. **Will you help us reach these people?**

Extend this ministry by sowing three, five, ten, or *even more* books today and change people's lives for the better! Your generosity will be part of catalyzing the Great Awakening that many have been prophesying and praying for.